Reunion Solutions Planner

Organize and Manage Your
Reunion with Checklists, Ideas,
Budgets and Worksheets

Reunion Solutions Planner:

Organize and Manage Your Reunion with Checklists, Ideas, Budgets and Worksheets

by Dina C Carson and Risa J Johnson

Published by:

Reunion Solutions Press
P.O. Box 999
Niwot, CO 80544
www.ReunionSolutions.com

Copyright © 2004 by Reunion Solutions Press
Printed in the United States of America
     ISBN 0-9724975-8-7
Cover Design by Robin R Meetz
     Imagination Technology, Inc. www.imaginationtechnology.com

Publisher's Cataloging-in-Publication Data

Carson, Dina C, 1961 -
Johnson, Risa J, 1960 -

Reunion Solutions Planner:
Organize and Manage Your Reunion with Checklists,
Ideas, Budgets and Worksheets

       p.   cm.
     Includes index.
     ISBN 0-9724975-8-7   LOC
      1. Reunions—Planning.
2. United States—Social life and customs.
3. Family Reunions—United States—Planning
4. Class Reunions—Handbooks—Planning
5. Military Reunions—Handbooks—Planning   I. Title.
LB 3618.C3212 2004
394.2 Car

Table of Contents

Reunion Solutions Planner

Part 4   Reunion Operating Systems: Gathering Data

Part 5 — Gathering a Crowd: Promoting the Reunion

Table of Contents

Reunion Solutions Planner

Table of Contents

Part 8 — Nearing the Finish Line: Enjoying the Fruits of Your Labor

Reunion Solutions Planner

Chapter 1

Together Again ...:
Planning a Reunion

 very year in the United States, over half a million reunions take place — from coast to coast, in small towns, in rural areas and in big cities. Reunions are exciting! They're a chance to reconnect with the people who are important to us. They're a chance to remember our common past and celebrate the lives we're leading now. Reunions are about our shared experiences. They're about a group and its culture, our continuity and our collective identities. They're about our shared experiences in the past and our common experiences in the present. They're also about creating new memories.

School reunions are primarily about nostalgia, curiosity and reconnecting. They help members recall and celebrate a brief period of time.

Family reunions are foremost about celebrating a collective identity — a lasting membership in a tightknit group. Many families have a long history that reaches back generations or even centuries.

Military service is characterized by courage, loyalty, honor and tradition, so military groups look back to their shared experiences and celebrate the strongest and most powerful relationships they've established.

Corporate groups often celebrate teamwork, success or careers and association reunions focus on common interests.

Reunions gather families, reunite classmates, salute veterans, celebrate business success and renew ties between members of associations.

What's not to love about a reunion?

Register your reunion on our website ... FREE!

ReunionSolutions.com

REUNION ADVICE ONLINE

everything you need to plan an extraordinary family, school, military, corporate or association reunion

- Home
- The Books
- Ask Us
- Quick Help
- Share Ideas
- Reunions
- Resource Center

- Register a Reunion
- Online Store

- New Vendor Account
- Member Login

- Press Room
- Distributors

Come register your reunion on our website!

- You'll have access to your account 24/7
- Change it as often as you like
- Announce your committee meetings
- List your contact information
- Keep your group members up-to-date
- Announce your reunion dates
- Describe your events
- Publish your ticket prices
- Advertise your souvenirs
- Post directions
- Offer incentives to attend
- Jumpstart your publicity
- Post instructions for submitting Reunion Book information
- Ask members to contribute memorabilia
- Let members know you need their help

Chapter 2

What if I Don't Know Anyone?: Myths, Misconceptions and Challenges

 et us dispel some of the myths about planning reunions.

How Hard Can it Be? One of the biggest challenges to a *successful* reunion is not having a plan. While it's possible to just muddle along, it's a much more efficient use of your committee people and your time if you develop a plan then carry it out. Forging ahead without a plan is also one of the biggest obstacles to a *creative* reunion. The most creative reunions focus on the group that's gathering, its history and traditions.

"It's not that different from a wedding." Well, it's not that different from a wedding except there's no bride, no groom and no fussy wedding coordinator quoting wedding etiquette. More seriously, reunions *are* similar to weddings except for what's meaningful. What guests will do at the reunion is what makes it different from any old gathering.

"Cheaper is better." Wrong. Cheap is just cheap. Besides, cheaper is not the point. Value is the point. An extraordinary reunion is worth the money.

"We don't need more than a couple of people to plan this." A couple of super human people, maybe. We're hoping you have Superman and Wonder Woman on speed dial. For us mere mortals, an effective, efficient committee is more than just a few people.

"A few e-mails will do it." If a few e-mails would do it, businesses wouldn't advertise during the Super Bowl. Hold on. We're not talking about running television commercials. What we *are* talking about is doing whatever's necessary to get people to the reunion.

What's Your Excuse for not coming to the Reunion?

Chapter 3

A Call to Arms:
Jumpstart Your Reunion

he most common question we get from reunion planners is: "Where do we start?" That's a good question because you could get started doing any one of a number of things and be on the right track. The biggest jumpstart you can give yourselves is a good review of the big picture — to get a handle on the major areas so you can break them down into smaller steps. Once you identify the steps, you can set deadlines so that all the pieces come together on time. Where to begin is a lot like baking a cake; you have to gather the right ingredients before you can get started, and we've found a recipe that works.

Most committees start planning about 12 to 18 months before the reunion and it's helpful to look at the project as a whole before you break it down into parts. First you need to know how far you have to go and how much time you have to get there. Once you have an idea of the scope of the project, you can gauge how much help you need to manage it.

Businesses use project management to help focus on priorities, track performance, overcome difficulties and adapt to change. Good project management will help you develop the best team you can, guide it in the right direction and ensure that members benefit from the experience. We've found that the basic principles of project management work for reunions, too.

In this chapter you'll find information and calendars to give you a look at an overall reunion plan so you can begin mapping out your reunion.

18 Month Timeline Calendar

		1
Payment Deadline →		2
		3
Send the Invitation		4
→		5
		6
Hold a Budget Meeting		7
→		8
		9
Establish the Grand Plan		10
		11
→		12
		13
		14
		15
		16
		17
		18

18 Month At-a-Look Calendar

16	13	10	
17	14	11	
18	15	12	Notes

7

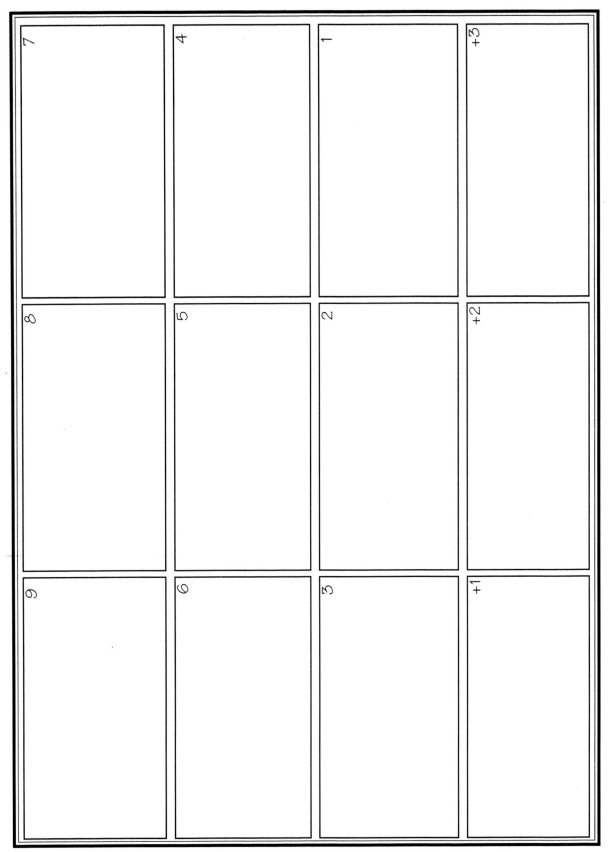

Project Plan Calendar

Kickoff Communique	Teaser Mailer	Invitation Mailing	Before the Deadline

The Eight Weeks Before the Reunion	Immediately Before the Reunion

Task Tracker

Task	Month 18	Month 17	Month 16	Month 15	Month 14	Month 13	Month 12	Month 11	Month 10

Task	Month 9	Month 8	Month 7	Month 6	Month 5	Month 4	Month 3	Month 2	Month 1

Chapter 4

Marshalling the Troops:
Organizing an Effective Committee

One way to ensure an especially memorable experience during your reunion is to be involved in the planning. As a member of the committee you'll have a say in the choice of events, get a sneak preview of pictures, letters, news, gossip and other intriguing bits of information ahead of everyone else! Sound like fun? Who *wouldn't* want to be on the planning committee, you say? Well, organizing a spectacular reunion — even a small one — takes time and commitment.

Even if you're planning a small reunion, you'll probably need an Executive Committee to take care of the basics — event organizing, managing committee meetings, accounting, invitations, communications and record keeping. We use the title *Chairman* for each of the Executive Committee positions. Larger reunions may need *Project Coordinators* to handle specific duties such as a Reunion Book, entertainment, videography, photography, memorabilia or memorials. You'll probably also have people who won't want to be members of the Executive Committee or Project Coordinators, but will want to be involved in the decision-making as *Committee-Members-at-Large*. And no reunion would be complete without *Volunteers* and *Contributors*. While volunteers and contributors may not be actual members of the committee, they will help you from time to time as you're planning and again during the reunion.

In this chapter you'll find information to help you organize a committee, show you how group dynamics affect committees, suggest how your committee can establish its own ground rules and tips for streamlining committee communications and meeting management.

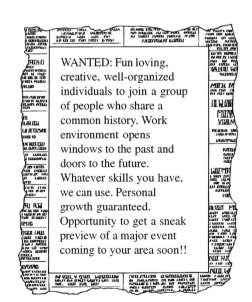

WANTED: Fun loving, creative, well-organized individuals to join a group of people who share a common history. Work environment opens windows to the past and doors to the future. Whatever skills you have, we can use. Personal growth guaranteed. Opportunity to get a sneak preview of a major event coming to your area soon!!

Problems? Questions? Concerns? Ask us, maybe can help!

ReunionSolutions.com

everything you need to plan an extraordinary family, school, military, corporate or association reunion

- Home
- The Books
- Ask Us
- Quick Help
- Share Ideas
- Reunions
- Resource Center

- Register a Reunion
- Online Store

- New Vendor Account
- Member Login

- Press Room
- Distributors

Tell us the problem, maybe we can solve it!

- Having a hard time finding just what you need in your area?
- Need a theme idea?
- Can't find a photographer?
- Have a question about designing your website?
- Don't know how to layout your Reunion Book?
- Need a souvenir idea?
- Can't settle on a menu?
- Need a suggestion for a facility?
- Need a reunion coordinator?
- Want to find a concierge?
- Need some help locating memorabilia?
- Need an investigator to help locate your members?
- Have a questions about creating a multimedia presentation?
- Having trouble with a vendor?

(Tell us the specifics. We'll call the business and see if we can get a resolution for you.)

Effective Meeting Checklist

Executive Committee Chairman Role Reminders

- [ ] Start the meeting at the announced time
- [ ] Adhere to the committee's ground rules
- [ ] Watch for common time wasters
- [ ] Keep the meeting moving forward
- [ ] Encourage participation from everyone
- [ ] Wrap up by briefly summarizing decisions and actions to be taken
- [ ] Get the Meeting Record to prepare an e-mail meeting summary
- [ ] Conduct a post-meeting evaluation

Meeting Essentials

- [ ] New Member Catch-Up Sheet
- [ ] Agenda
- [ ] Pre-start activities (Post-meeting activities)
- [ ] Committee Calendar
- [ ] Membership list and information

Meeting Supplies

- [ ] Flip charts
- [ ] White board
- [ ] Markers
- [ ] Tape
- [ ] Sticky notes
- [ ] Note paper
- [ ] Pens
- [ ] Paper
- [ ] Kush balls™
- [ ] Stapler/staples

Committee Ground Rules

We will assume positive intent

We will assume positive intent when communicating with each other, whether it's during a committee meeting, by memo or by e-mail. Misstatements can lead to misunderstandings and most of the time a simple clarification can straighten things out.

We will commit to attend meetings

It's difficult to maintain continuity if committee members are absent when important decisions are being made. Reunion plans are interdependent and the absence of one or two committee members can affect the work of others.

We will be honest about our other commitments

We all have busy lives and have other obligations but we won't to make promises regarding the reunion unless we can deliver.

We will complete assigned tasks

Some tasks are so large and so important that they need to be spread out among the entire committee. These tasks will be important to the success of our reunion, but they won't be successful unless everyone follows through.

We will keep each other up to date on our progress

Each committee member will be responsible for reporting their progress to the group. No project in a reunion plan exists in a vacuum and often the progress of one part affects the next step. It's important that we are prepared to report our status at every meeting.

We will have an understanding of how our part fits into the whole

Each member will make an effort to understand how our project's progress, lack of progress or changes will affect the work of others.

We will ask for help if we need it

We will ask for help if it's needed and we will be specific about what we need. There's no need to gear up a bunch of people to help if only a few are needed.

We will respect each other's responsibilities

We will not make end-runs or make changes in each other's areas. Even if the effort is well-intended, it often creates conflict and may lead to misunderstandings.

We will avoid creating additional work for each other

Don't expect special privileges if it will create more work for a fellow committee member. If there's a rule or a deadline in place, stick to it.

We will speak up if something or someone is creating more work for us

We will let each other know if we're making our jobs more difficult. Information like this, kept to one's self, causes hard feelings.

We will not play the blame game

A task as complicated as planning a reunion is bound to suffer some mistakes. Stuff happens. We will not spend time pointing fingers. We will spend our time trying to find solutions.

We will not back stab

If you have a problem with another committee member, work it out that person. We will not spread strife throughout the committee by trying to win others to our side of an argument.

We will maintain confidences

If information is shared in confidence, we will not pass it along to others. Reunion issues are public, personal issues are not. Once a trust is broken, it's hard to get it back.

We will stay in touch

Once we have an agreement about how we'll communicate with each other, each of us will be responsible for keeping up. That way, no one will miss out on regular communications.

Don't use e-mail for spam

We will not send each other chain mail, spam, forwarded mail or 'thought for the day' stuff. We will save e-mail communications for things related to the reunion.

Committee Meeting Agenda Planner

Meeting date	Meeting place
Meeting start time	Approximate length

Meeting goals summary

Executive Committee

	informa-tional	problem-solving	decision-making
Executive Committee Chairman _____			
Updates _____			
New agenda items _____	☐	☐	☐
Accountant _____			
Updates _____			
New agenda items _____	☐	☐	☐
Record Keeper _____			
Updates _____			
New agenda items _____	☐	☐	☐
Communications Czar _____			
Updates _____			
New agenda items _____	☐	☐	☐
Event Chairman _____			
Updates _____			
New agenda items _____	☐	☐	☐
Event Chairman _____			
Updates _____			
New agenda items _____	☐	☐	☐
Event Chairman _____			
Updates _____			
New agenda items _____	☐	☐	☐
Event Chairman _____			
Updates _____			
New agenda items _____	☐	☐	☐
Event Chairman _____			
Updates _____			
New agenda items _____	☐	☐	☐

Committee Meeting Agenda Planner

Project Coordinators

	informa-tional	problem-solving	decision-making

Volunteer Coordinator _____
    Updates _____
    New agenda items _____
	☐	☐	☐

Amenities Coordinator_____
    Updates _____
    New agenda items _____
	☐	☐	☐

Fund-raising Coordinator_____
    Updates _____
    New agenda items _____
	☐	☐	☐

Member Search Coordinator_____
    Updates _____
    New agenda items _____
	☐	☐	☐

Website Coordinator _____
    Updates _____
    New agenda items _____
	☐	☐	☐

Memorabilia Coordinator_____
    Updates _____
    New agenda items _____
	☐	☐	☐

Memorials Coordinator_____
    Updates _____
    New agenda items _____
	☐	☐	☐

Presentation Coordinator_____
    Updates _____
    New agenda items _____
	☐	☐	☐

Music Coordinator_____
    Updates _____
    New agenda items _____
	☐	☐	☐

Decorations Coordinator_____
    Updates _____
    New agenda items _____
	☐	☐	☐

Souvenirs Coordinator _____
    Updates _____
    New agenda items _____
	☐	☐	☐

Reunion Book Coordinator _____
    Updates _____
    New agenda items _____
	☐	☐	☐

CD-ROM Coordinator_____
    Updates _____
    New agenda items _____
	☐	☐	☐

Videography Coordinator _____
    Updates _____
    New agenda items _____
	☐	☐	☐

Photography Coordinator _____
    Updates _____
    New agenda items _____
	☐	☐	☐

Questions for the ECC _____

Other business_____

Next meeting date and time _____

Expect meeting followup (date)_____

Committee Meeting Record

Meeting date	Meeting place
Meeting start time	Approximate length

Meeting goals summary		informa-tional	problem-solving	decision-making
Accountant		☐	☐	☐
Record Keeper		☐	☐	☐
Communications Czar		☐	☐	☐
Event Chairman		☐	☐	☐
Event Chairman		☐	☐	☐
Event Chairman		☐	☐	☐
Event Chairman		☐	☐	☐

Questions for the ECC

Other business

Next meeting date and time

	informa-tional	problem-solving	decision-making
Volunteer Coordinator	☐	☐	☐
Amenities Coordinator	☐	☐	☐
Fund-raising Coordinator	☐	☐	☐
Member Search Coordinator	☐	☐	☐
Website Coordinator	☐	☐	☐
Memorabilia Coordinator	☐	☐	☐
Memorials Coordinator	☐	☐	☐
Presentation Coordinator	☐	☐	☐
Music Coordinator	☐	☐	☐
Decorations Coordinator	☐	☐	☐
Souvenirs Coordinator	☐	☐	☐
Reunion Book Coordinator	☐	☐	☐
CD-ROM Coordinator	☐	☐	☐
Videography Coordinator	☐	☐	☐
Photography Coordinator	☐	☐	☐

New Member Information Sheet

The committee's vision of the upcoming reunion

Our Grand Plan — plans and progress to date

Committee roster

How you can plan a role in the meeting today

Jobs that still need to be filled

Committee's self-governing rules

E-mail Meeting Reminder

E-mail tips
- Correct distribution list
- Descriptive subject line
- Forewarn recipients of large attachments
- Include contact information in the signature
- Let committee members know what to expect from the upcoming meeting
- Be specific in asking for responses

Next meeting date

Next meeting time

Next meeting place

Simplified meeting agenda

What committee members should bring to the meeting

Meeting Follow Up

Synopsis of decisions

Synopsis of new assignments

Synopsis of areas where help is still needed

Next Meeting Date	
Next Meeting Time	
Next Meeting Place	

Chairman's Task Sheet

Jan	Feb	Mar	Apr
May	June	July	Aug
Sept	Oct	Nov	Dec

Check Current Month

Task Description	
Deadline	
Committee Action Needed	
Subcommittee Action Needed	
Subcommittee Members for This Task	
Name	Phone
Name	Phone
Name	Phone
Name	Phone
Name	Phone

Task Description	
Deadline	
Committee Action Needed	
Subcommittee Action Needed	
Subcommittee Members for This Task	
Name	Phone
Name	Phone
Name	Phone
Name	Phone
Name	Phone

Task Description	
Deadline	
Committee Action Needed	
Subcommittee Action Needed	
Subcommittee Members for This Task	
Name	Phone
Name	Phone
Name	Phone
Name	Phone
Name	Phone

Task Description	
Deadline	
Committee Action Needed	
Subcommittee Action Needed	
Subcommittee Members for This Task	
Name	Phone
Name	Phone
Name	Phone
Name	Phone
Name	Phone

Task Description	
Deadline	
Committee Action Needed	
Subcommittee Action Needed	
Subcommittee Members for This Task	
Name	Phone
Name	Phone
Name	Phone
Name	Phone
Name	Phone

Task Description	
Deadline	
Committee Action Needed	
Subcommittee Action Needed	
Subcommittee Members for This Task	
Name	Phone
Name	Phone
Name	Phone
Name	Phone
Name	Phone

Task Description	
Deadline	
Committee Action Needed	
Subcommittee Action Needed	
Subcommittee Members for This Task	
Name	Phone
Name	Phone
Name	Phone
Name	Phone
Name	Phone

Monthly Committee Tasks

Jan	Feb	Mar	Apr
May	June	July	Aug
Sept	Oct	Nov	Dec

Check Current Month

Executive Committee Chairman

Project List	Deadline

Accountant

Project List	Deadline

Record Keeper

Project List	Deadline

Communications Czar

Project List	Deadline

Event Chairman

Project List	Deadline

Event Chairman

Project List	Deadline

Event Chairman

Project List	Deadline

Sub-Committee Members List

Accountant

Name	Phone
Name	Phone
Name	Phone
Name	Phone
Name	Phone

Record Keeper

Name	Phone
Name	Phone
Name	Phone
Name	Phone
Name	Phone

Communications Czar

Name	Phone
Name	Phone
Name	Phone
Name	Phone
Name	Phone

Event Chairman

Name	Phone
Name	Phone
Name	Phone
Name	Phone
Name	Phone

Event Chairman

Name	Phone
Name	Phone
Name	Phone
Name	Phone
Name	Phone

Event Chairman

Name	Phone
Name	Phone
Name	Phone
Name	Phone

Subcommittee Name:

Name	Phone
Name	Phone
Name	Phone
Name	Phone
Name	Phone

Subcommittee Name:

Name	Phone
Name	Phone
Name	Phone
Name	Phone
Name	Phone

Subcommittee Name:

Name	Phone
Name	Phone
Name	Phone
Name	Phone
Name	Phone

Subcommittee Name:

Name	Phone
Name	Phone
Name	Phone
Name	Phone
Name	Phone

Subcommittee Name:

Name	Phone
Name	Phone
Name	Phone
Name	Phone
Name	Phone

Subcommittee Name:

Name	Phone
Name	Phone
Name	Phone
Name	Phone
Name	Phone

Chapter 5

Great Expectations:
Defining Success

 efining your reunion is a little like using a map for a lengthy road trip. While it's not necessary to memorize each and every turn in the highway before you depart, wise travelers plot a general course before getting into the car. The same thing is true of reunion planning. A plan is a must.

One of the first things you should discuss is what will constitute success in the eyes of your committee. The answers to the following questions will help establish your unique definition of success. Having a framework to refer back to will help manage the committee's expectations when deciding what each event will look like, feel like, taste like, smell like and sound like.

Who's on your guest list? Just who are you planning this party for? How many people do you expect? What will the reunion consist of? What's your definition of success? How many days will it last? Where will you hold it? When will you hold it? How will you let members know you're having a reunion? How will you pay for it? What makes this a reunion and not a business gathering?

By spending some time defining a successful reunion, you'll be able to work smarter not harder when it comes to choosing vendors, making reservations, creating decorations or selecting a facility.

In this chapter you'll find some guidelines for defining your reunion, starting with a definition of what will constitute success in the eyes of your committee. Having a framework to refer back to will help manage the your expectations when deciding what each event will look like, feel like, taste like, smell like and sound like.

Choosing a Geographic Location Checklist

City: _____

Chamber of Commerce: _____ Phone: _____

State/City Tourist Board: _____ Phone: _____

What is the city's peak tourist season? _____

Which airlines serve the city? _____ Train service _____

What type of public transportation is available? _____

How distant is the airport and train station(s) from hotels? _____

What recreation facilities are available? _____

Local Events taking place? _____
_____
_____
_____
_____

Tourist attractions in the area? _____
_____
_____
_____
_____

Entertainment in the area? _____
_____
_____
_____
_____
_____

Hotels/Motels in the area? _____
_____
_____
_____

Restaurants in the area? _____
_____
_____
_____

Chapter 6

Grand Plans:
Designing Your Reunion

*I*t's been our observation that when it comes to reunion schedules there seems to be some kind of unwritten rule requiring they all be cookie-cutter images of each other — a cocktail party followed by a dinner dance followed by a picnic. We've checked ... there's no such rule! Before you get started throwing ideas into the ring for consideration, take a look at what's possible in the greater universe of event planning.

Put on your thinking caps and let your imaginations take over. There are literally hundreds of events and event combinations from which to choose — events with a theme, food events, contests, tours, displays, presentations, in-town fairs, outdoor activities, sightseeing — whatever! Add a display, a presentation, entertainment or group activities. Remember when we suggested that the most successful reunions were the ones that did something to make the reunion specifically about the members of your group? Add memorabilia. Memorabilia from will establish the reunion as 'uniquely yours.' Anything you can dream up can be included in your reunion. There's so much to choose from it's staggering.

In this chapter you find information to help you build upon the decisions you made while defining success — the general do's and don'ts for choosing reunion events and plenty of options to choose from. Create an outline of the schedule, a sketch for each event, refine the details, choose the vendors and finally create your Grand Plan, the wish list of all the things you could want in a reunion.

Theme Coordination Checklist

Theme Description

Decorating plan

Tables

Floor

Walls

Ceiling

3D

Invitation ideas

Refreshments

Suggested attire

Souvenirs

Music/background sound

Event Summary

Description

Idea Sketch

Facility

Food

Beverages

Memorabilia

Souvenirs

Presentation(s)

Music

Decorations

Event Summary

Description

Idea Sketch

Facility

Food

Beverages

Memorabilia

Souvenirs

Presentation(s)

Music

Decorations

Day Summary

7 AM	7:30 AM	8 AM	8:30	9 AM	9:30 AM	10 AM	10:30 AM	11 AM	Noon	12:30 AM	1 PM	1:30 PM	2 PM	2:30 PM	3 PM	3:30 PM	4 PM	4:30 PM	5 PM	5:30 PM	6 PM	6:30 PM	7 PM	7:30 PM	8 PM	8:30 PM	9 PM	9:30 PM	10 PM	10:30 PM	11 PM	11:30 PM	Midnight	12:30 AM	1 AM

Day Summary

7 AM	7:30 AM	8 AM	8:30 AM	9 AM	9:30 AM	10 AM	10:30 AM	11 AM	Noon	12:30 AM	1 PM	1:30 PM	2 PM	2:30 PM	3 PM	3:30 PM	4 PM	4:30 PM	5 PM	5:30 PM	6 PM	6:30 PM	7 PM	7:30 PM	8 PM	8:30 PM	9 PM	9:30 PM	10 PM	10:30 PM	11 PM	11:30 PM	Midnight	12:30 AM	1 AM

Grand Plan Summary

Event 1 Summary

Date: _____
Start Time: _____
End Time: _____
Location: _____
Event Chairman:
_____

Event 2 Summary

Date: _____
Start Time: _____
End Time: _____
Location: _____
Event Chairman:
_____

Event 3 Summary

Date: _____
Start Time: _____
End Time: _____
Location: _____
Event Chairman:
_____

Event 4 Summary

Date: _____
Start Time: _____
End Time: _____
Location: _____
Event Chairman:
_____

Event 5 Summary

Date: _____
Start Time: _____
End Time: _____
Location: _____
Event Chairman:
_____

Grand Plan Summary

Event 6 Summary

Date: _____
Start Time: _____
End Time: _____
Location: _____
Event Chairman:
_____

Event 7 Summary

Date: _____
Start Time: _____
End Time: _____
Location: _____
Event Chairman:
_____

Event 8 Summary

Date: _____
Start Time: _____
End Time: _____
Location: _____
Event Chairman:
_____

Event 9 Summary

Date: _____
Start Time: _____
End Time: _____
Location: _____
Event Chairman:
_____

Event 10 Summary

Date: _____
Start Time: _____
End Time: _____
Location: _____
Event Chairman:
_____

Materials Checklist

Fund-raisers

Food Contests

Entries	Judges	Prizes	Business Entries

Arts and Crafts

Materials	Entries	Judges	Prizes

Sports Contest

Facility	Field	Equipment	Sign up
Judges	Uniforms Prizes		

Talent Contest

Sign up	Accompanists	AV Equipment
Judges	Prizes	

Dance Contest

Sign up	Musicians	Music
AV Equipment	Judges	Prizes

Trivia Contest

Sign up	Props	Judges
Prizes	Trivia	

Tours

Min/Max Number	Ticket prices	Group Rates
Tour Length	Travel Time To/From	Tour Guide

Bazaars/Trade Shows

Display Area	Display Tables	Table Dividers
Display Racks	Security	
Booth Maps	Exhibitor's Checklist	

Displays

Exhibits

Artifacts	Rented	Borrowed	Bought
Value	How to be displayed		
Display Equip	Security	Exhibitors	
Club	Contact		
Corporation	Contact		

Continuous Play Video/Movie Screening

Video	Monitor	VCR/DVD	Security

Slide Show/Multimedia Show

Slides/CD	Projector	Screen	Security

Photographs

Display space	Background
Borrowed	Returned

Materials Checklist

Activities

Class/Seminar

Instructor	Instructor Materials	Class Materials
AV Equipment		

Children's Program

Reader	Sing-along-leader	Accompanist

Crafts/Souvenir Assembly

Materials	Distribution	Instructions

Group Photograph

Wide Format Camera	Ladder/Risers	Lighting
Assembly Area		

Awards Presentation

Sound System	Podium	Awards

Skits

Stage	Sound System	Lighting	Props

Presentations

Welcome and Announcements

Microphone	Amplifier/Bullhorn	Podium

Slideshow

Projector	Screen/Monitor	Sound System

Video Clips

Clips from Members	Editing Equipment	Videocamera
Screen/Monitor	VCR/DVD Player	Sound System

Speaker

Sound system	Podium	AV Equipment	Talking Points

Toast

Champagne	Sound System	Emcee

Optional Activities

Theatre/Amusement Park/Tourist Attractions

Reservations	Ticket Pickup	Parking Map
Travel Time To/From	Suggested Clothing	Transportation

Major League Sports

Reservations	Parking Map	
Transportation	Travel Time To/From	

Special Showing

IMAX	Planetarium	Movie
Reservations	Parking Map	
Travel Time To/From	Transportation	

Chapter 7

Headhunting:
Expanding the Committee, Hiring Vendors

nce you have a Grand Plan, you may need more than just an Executive Committee to carry it out — you may need some Project Coordinators. Project Coordinators have more specific duties than members of the Executive Committee do.

The Amenities Coordinator (*see Chapter 9: the Budget*) will act like the concierge for the reunion.

The Fund-raising Coordinator (*see Chapter 9: the Budget*) will raise a few dollars if you get into a budget crunch.

The Member Search Coordinator (*see Chapter 11: Member Search*) will conduct the member search and help keep track of the information.

The Volunteer Coordinator (*see Chapters 13: Invitations, Chapter 29: Walk-Through and Chapter 30: At the Reunion*) will recruit, schedule and train volunteers.

The Website Coordinator (*see Chapter 15: Website*) will design the website or find a web designer and establish a relationship with an ISP.

The Memorabilia Coordinator (*see Chapter 19: Memorabilia*) will gather mementos from the past, obtain memorabilia for as decorations and help compile information for the Reunion Book.

The Memorials Coordinator (*see Chapter 20: Memorials*) will plan memorials and contact deceased members' families to invite their participation.

The Presentation Coordinator (*see Chapter 21: Presentations*) will create multimedia presentations, work with an emcee and hire speakers or entertainers.

The Music Coordinator (*see Chapter 22: Music*) will find musicians or arrange for recorded music and any copyright permissions you might need.

The Decorations Coordinator (*see Chapter 23: Decorations*) should be someone who can envision the look, the atmosphere and the feel of the events.

The Souvenir Coordinator (*see Chapter 24: Souvenirs*) will locate, create, market and distribute souvenirs.

The Reunion Book Coordinator (*see Chapter 25: Reunion Book*) will design, lay out and ready the manuscript for a book printer or find a graphic designer who can.

The CD-ROM Coordinator (*see Chapter 26: CD-ROM*) will lay out, design and reproduce a CD-ROM or find a multimedia designer who can.

The Videography Coordinator (*see Chapter 27: Videography*) will shoot and edit raw footage into a finished video or find a videographer who can.

The Photography Coordinator (*see Chapter 28: Photography*) will take group photographs and candids or find a photographer who can.

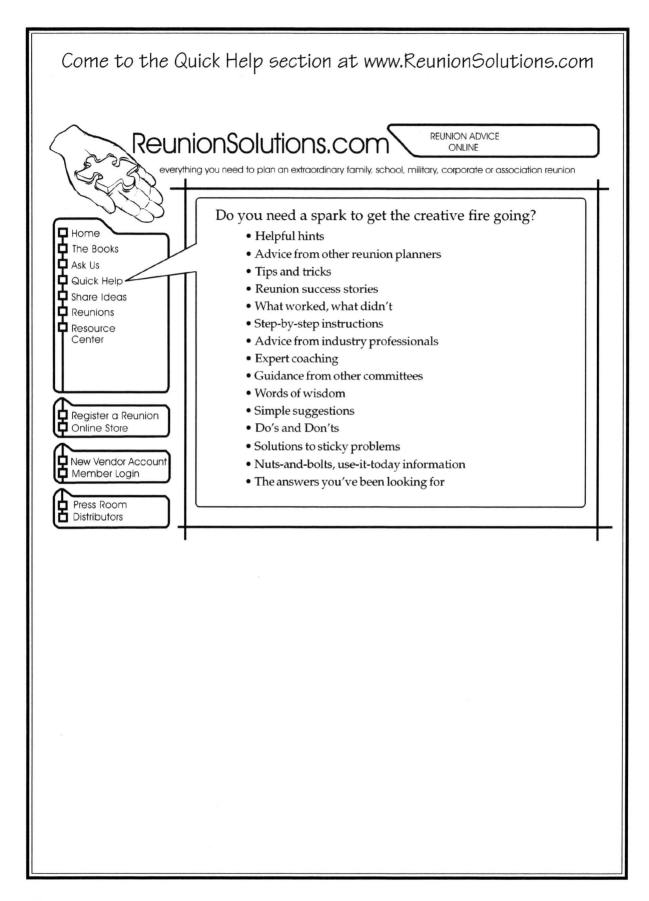

ReunionSolutions.com

REUNION ADVICE
ONLINE

everything you need to plan an extraordinary family, school, military, corporate or association reunion

Home
The Books
Ask Us
Quick Help
Share Ideas
Reunions
Resource
Center

Register a Reunion
Online Store

New Vendor Account
Member Login

Press Room
Distributors

Do you need a spark to get the creative fire going?

- Helpful hints
- Advice from other reunion planners
- Tips and tricks
- Reunion success stories
- What worked, what didn't
- Step-by-step instructions
- Advice from industry professionals
- Expert coaching
- Guidance from other committees
- Words of wisdom
- Simple suggestions
- Do's and Don'ts
- Solutions to sticky problems
- Nuts-and-bolts, use-it-today information
- The answers you've been looking for

Project Coordinator's Task Sheet

Jan	Feb	Mar	Apr
May	June	July	Aug
Sept	Oct	Nov	Dec

——— Check Current Month

Task Description

Deadline
Committee Action Needed
Subcommittee Action Needed
Subcommittee Members for This Task

Name	Phone
Name	Phone
Name	Phone
Name	Phone
Name	Phone

Task Description

Deadline
Committee Action Needed
Subcommittee Action Needed
Subcommittee Members for This Task

Name	Phone
Name	Phone
Name	Phone
Name	Phone
Name	Phone

Task Description

Deadline
Committee Action Needed
Subcommittee Action Needed
Subcommittee Members for This Task

Name	Phone
Name	Phone
Name	Phone
Name	Phone

Task Description	
Deadline	
Committee Action Needed	
Subcommittee Action Needed	
Subcommittee Members for This Task	
Name	Phone
Name	Phone
Name	Phone
Name	Phone
Name	Phone

Task Description	
Deadline	
Committee Action Needed	
Subcommittee Action Needed	
Subcommittee Members for This Task	
Name	Phone
Name	Phone
Name	Phone
Name	Phone
Name	Phone

Task Description	
Deadline	
Committee Action Needed	
Subcommittee Action Needed	
Subcommittee Members for This Task	
Name	Phone
Name	Phone
Name	Phone
Name	Phone
Name	Phone

Task Description	
Deadline	
Committee Action Needed	
Subcommittee Action Needed	
Subcommittee Members for This Task	
Name	Phone
Name	Phone
Name	Phone
Name	Phone

Vendor Contact Sheet

Vendor Name	Vendor Service	
Address		
Contact Name		Phone
Emergency Contact		Phone
Notes		

Vendor Name	Vendor Service	
Address		
Contact Name		Phone
Emergency Contact		Phone
Notes		

Vendor Name	Vendor Service	
Address		
Contact Name		Phone
Emergency Contact		Phone
Notes		

Vendor Name	Vendor Service	
Address		
Contact Name		Phone
Emergency Contact		Phone
Notes		

Vendor Name	Vendor Service	
Address		
Contact Name		Phone
Emergency Contact		Phone
Notes		

Vendor Name	Vendor Service	
Address		
Contact Name		Phone
Emergency Contact		Phone
Notes		

Vendor Name	Vendor Service	
Address		
Contact Name		Phone
Emergency Contact		Phone
Notes		

Vendor Contact Sheet

Vendor Name	Vendor Service	
Address		
Contact Name		Phone
Emergency Contact		Phone
Notes		

Vendor Name	Vendor Service	
Address		
Contact Name		Phone
Emergency Contact		Phone
Notes		

Vendor Name	Vendor Service	
Address		
Contact Name		Phone
Emergency Contact		Phone
Notes		

Vendor Name	Vendor Service	
Address		
Contact Name		Phone
Emergency Contact		Phone
Notes		

Vendor Name	Vendor Service	
Address		
Contact Name		Phone
Emergency Contact		Phone
Notes		

Vendor Name	Vendor Service	
Address		
Contact Name		Phone
Emergency Contact		Phone
Notes		

Vendor Name	Vendor Service	
Address		
Contact Name		Phone
Emergency Contact		Phone
Notes		

Volunteer Assignment Sheet

Volunteer
Task Volunteered For
Response Card Sent (date)
Volunteer
Task Volunteered For
Response Card Sent (date)
Volunteer
Task Volunteered For
Response Card Sent (date)
Volunteer
Task Volunteered For
Response Card Sent (date)
Volunteer
Task Volunteered For
Response Card Sent (date)
Volunteer
Task Volunteered For
Response Card Sent (date)
Volunteer
Task Volunteered For
Response Card Sent (date)
Volunteer
Task Volunteered For
Response Card Sent (date)
Volunteer
Task Volunteered For
Response Card Sent (date)
Volunteer
Task Volunteered For
Response Card Sent (date)
Volunteer
Task Volunteered For
Response Card Sent (date)
Volunteer
Task Volunteered For
Response Card Sent (date)

Sub-Committee Calling Chain

Project Coordinator

Name	Phone
Name	Phone
Name	Phone
Name	Phone
Name	Phone

Project Coordinator

Name	Phone
Name	Phone
Name	Phone
Name	Phone
Name	Phone

Project Coordinator

Name	Phone
Name	Phone
Name	Phone
Name	Phone
Name	Phone

Project Coordinator

Name	Phone
Name	Phone
Name	Phone
Name	Phone
Name	Phone

Project Coordinator

Name	Phone
Name	Phone
Name	Phone
Name	Phone
Name	Phone

Project Coordinator

Name	Phone
Name	Phone
Name	Phone
Name	Phone

Chapter 8

The Next Best Thing to Being There:
The Virtual Reunion

$\mathcal{S}$ometimes there are enough obstacles to holding a full reunion that a virtual reunion is a good alternative.

As we age, it may become difficult to meet in person. Members of a 75-year school reunion, for example, would all be in their 90s. While they might not be able to meet with each other, younger generations could create a virtual reunion on behalf of these classmates by creating a Reunion Book or a video journal that would be shared with all remaining members of the class. As our World War II generation ages, more military groups might look to a virtual reunion to record their legacies for generations to come.

Some groups might have reunions only every few years and want to keep in touch between reunions. A virtual reunion would work well for this. Virtual reunions allow your group to reunite without having to travel.

Just because you're from an electronic generation, doesn't mean you should go entirely electronic and avoid having actual reunions or that the basic rules for all reunions don't apply. Even virtual reunions should focus on the common history and memories of the group and include the memorabilia that makes your group unique.

If you can't meet in person, generate some ideas for a virtual meeting — on paper, in a multimedia environment or electronically.

In this chapter you find ideas for virtual reunions — partial reunions, paper reunions, multimedia reunions or electronic reunions.

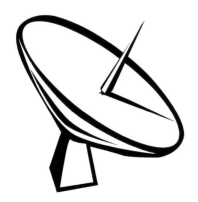

Virtual Reunions Checklist

Travel Reunions

- [ ] Transportation Arrangements
- [ ] Departure/Arrival Information
- [ ] Meeting Places and Times
- [ ] Accommodations List
- [ ] Tour Itinerary
- [ ] Travelers' Contact Information

Round Robin Letter Reunions

- [ ] Distribution Circle
- [ ] Timeline
- [ ] Labels
- [ ] Pass Along Instructions

Videoconference Reunions

- [ ] Videoconference Center
- [ ] Practice with the Equipment
- [ ] Emcee
- [ ] Remote Site Hookups
- [ ] Adapt Presentations for the Medium
- [ ] Invitations with Time and Place

E-Group Reunions

- [ ] Establish E-Group address
- [ ] Moderator
- [ ] Participation Requirements
- [ ] Customize E-Group site page
- [ ] Establish Communication Archive
- [ ] Construct E-Group Calendar
- [ ] Invite Participation

Newsgroup Reunions

- [ ] Newsgroup Application
- [ ] Moderator
- [ ] Participation Rules
- [ ] Participant List

Scrapbook Reunions

- [ ] Scrapbook Materials
- [ ] Distribution List
- [ ] Scrapbook Instruction Sheet
- [ ] Vendor for Color Copies
- [ ] Book Binder

Chapter 9

Money Matters:
Accounting and the Budget

lmost everyone has experience with a household budget or a budget for a wedding, but reunion budgets are *very* different. In a household budget, you know how much you have to spend and in a wedding budget, you know who's paying, but when budgeting for a reunion you won't have a firm estimate of how much money you'll be bringing in until long after you've made spending decisions. Not knowing how much money you'll have to work with is what causes reunion committees the most confusion when it comes to budgeting.

The first step is to discuss your expenses. Adding up the cost of using vendors will give you an estimate of what your total expenses will be. Next, determine your ticket prices. In order to settle on a ticket price, you'll need to know the lowest amount you *must* charge per ticket in order to cover your expenses. If your ticket price equals your per-person breakeven cost, then your expenses will exactly *equal* your revenues — in other words, you'll break even. Once you determine the breakeven cost, you'll have to decide how much *over* that amount you'll actually charge.

If ticket prices seem way too high, there are ways to lessen the financial burden by cutting your expenses or raising your revenues.

As a last resort, consider scaling back your plans. You've got a Grand Plan you think will give you a spectacular reunion. Don't slash and burn it just to hold ticket prices down. Hang in there, this chapter is full of tips to avoid radically changing your plans just to cut costs.

Help other reunion planners with **your** 'tricks of the trade'

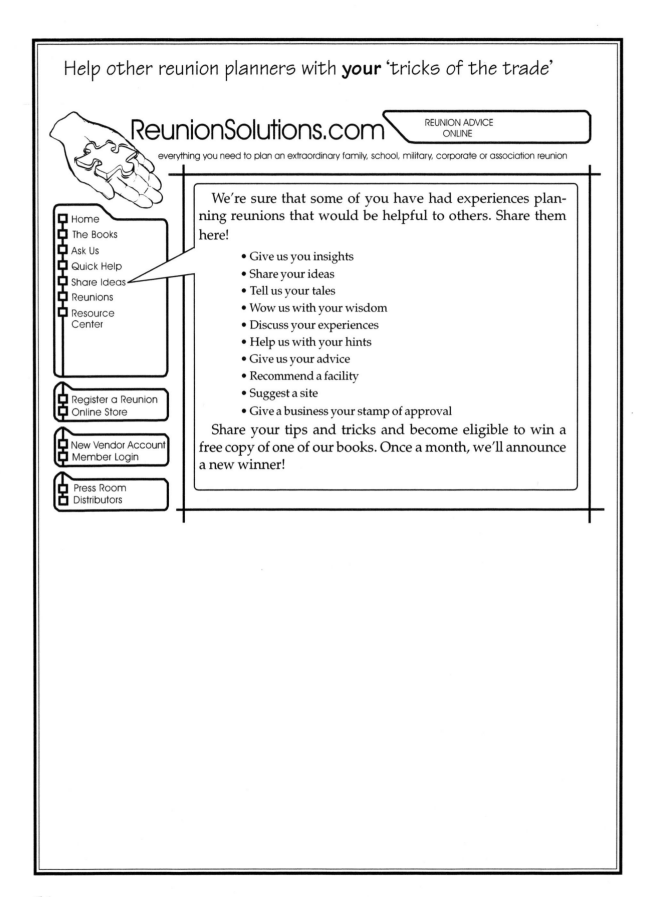

ReunionSolutions.com

REUNION ADVICE
ONLINE

everything you need to plan an extraordinary family, school, military, corporate or association reunion

Home
The Books
Ask Us
Quick Help
Share Ideas
Reunions
Resource Center

Register a Reunion
Online Store

New Vendor Account
Member Login

Press Room
Distributors

We're sure that some of you have had experiences planning reunions that would be helpful to others. Share them here!

- Give us you insights
- Share your ideas
- Tell us your tales
- Wow us with your wisdom
- Discuss your experiences
- Help us with your hints
- Give us your advice
- Recommend a facility
- Suggest a site
- Give a business your stamp of approval

Share your tips and tricks and become eligible to win a free copy of one of our books. Once a month, we'll announce a new winner!

Seed Money Record Sheet

	Gift	Loan	Amount	Applied to Ticket Price
Name				
Address				
Name				
Address				
Name				
Address				
Name				
Address				
Name				
Address				
Name				
Address				
Name				
Address				
Name				
Address				
Name				
Address				
Name				
Address				
Name				
Address				
Name				
Address				
Name				
Address				
Name				
Address				
Name				
Address				
Name				
Address				

Contributors Record Sheet

	Gift Description	Amount	Date Rec'd
Name			
Address			
Name			
Address			
Name			
Address			
Name			
Address			
Name			
Address			
Name			
Address			
Name			
Address			
Name			
Address			
Name			
Address			
Name			
Address			
Name			
Address			
Name			
Address			
Name			
Address			
Name			
Address			
Name			
Address			
Name			
Address			

Expense Ledger

Description of Expense	Date	Deposit	Date	Balance	Date	Deposit Returned

Committee Reimbursement Sheet

Expense	Committee Member	Date	Amount	Receipt

Daily Cost Ledger

Description

	Fixed Costs	Variable	Pay if you go
Facility			
Food			
Beverages			
Decorations			
Memorabilia			
Souvenirs			
Presentations			
Music			
Temporary Help			
Security			
Transportation			

Totals

Fixed costs

Divided by number of expected guests

Variable costs

☐ + ☐ = ☐

per-person cost

Breakeven Cost Worksheet

Fixed Costs

Divided by Estimated Attendance _____

Per-Person Fixed Cost

Variable Costs

Per-Person Variable Cost

Per-Person Breakeven Cost

Common Fixed and Variable Costs List	Fixed	Variable
Committee Expenses		
Committee communications	X	
Event Expenses		
Contests		
Materials/equipment/prizes/location fees	X	
Tours		
Tickets		X
Transportation	X	X
Tour guide	X	
Anteroom Events		
Displays/artifacts	X	
AV equipment rental/purchase	X	
Exhibit/speaker fees	X	
Class/seminar materials		X
Security	X	
Bazaars/Trade Shows		
Display tables/equipment	X	
Printed maps of participants	X	
Security	X	
Fund-raisers		
Prizes/products	X	
Marketing materials	X	
Locating Members		
Record keeping materials/software	X	
Search fees	X	X
Facility		
Room charges	X	
Cleanup/damage fees	X	
Food		
Meals		X
Utensils/serving dishes/tablecloths	X	
Service + gratuities	X	
Beverages		
Drinks		X
Service + Gratuities	X	
Condiments/Supplies	X	
Utensils/Glasses	X	
Publicity		
Printing/postage	X	
Publicist fees		
Mailings		
Printing/postage		X
Envelopes/labels/supplies		X
Design fees	X	
Memorabilia		
Reproduction costs		X
Artifact purchase/rental	X	
Memorials		
Memorial	X	
Permanent placement	X	

Common Fixed and Variable Costs List	Fixed	Variable
Reunion Book		
Layout/Design	X	
Printing/Binding		X
Souvenirs		
Design Costs	X	
Reproduction Costs	X	
Videography		
Videographer Fee	X	
Equipment Rental/Purchase	X	
Reproduction Costs		X
Mailing Costs		X
Photography		
Photographer Fee	X	
Equipment Rental/Purchase	X	
Reproduction Costs		X
Mailing Costs		X
Presentation		
AV Equipment Rental/Purchase	X	
Design/Development	X	
Awards	X	
Music		
Musician/DJ Fees	X	
Sound Equipment Rental/Purchase	X	
Copyright Payments	X	
Decorations		
Theme Materials	X	
Table Decorations	X	
Wall Decorations	X	
At the Reunion		
Registration Kit	X	
Registration Table Materials	X	
Welcome Signs	X	
After the Reunion		
Printing Costs		X
Mailing Costs		X
Transportation		
Tickets		X
Vehicle Rentals	X	
Security		
Personnel fees	X	
Tours		
Transportation Tickets		X
Lodging		X
Meals		X
Venue Tickets		X
Leader Materials	X	
Participant Materials		X

Chapter 10

Taming the Paper Tiger:
Record Keeping

ost reunion groups need to gather contact, personal and financial information.

Contact information is used primarily to help facilitate your mailings — name, address, city, state and zip code. Gathering your contact information will give you a launch point for your member search. Start with your entire member list. Create a record for each person on the list and start filling in the details.

You may also need to collect more *personal* information — information that may help you to locate a missing member by giving you a clue to the person's current whereabouts such as a name change, profession, employer, military service, spouse's name or schools attended. Any information that can provide you a clue for where to look next is helpful.

Compile information from registrations for the reunion. Tracking who has ordered and paid for what, will help you to know how many dinners or souvenirs to order. If the Record Keeper maintains information from registrations, it will be easy to cross-check the numbers with the Accountant before giving final numbers to vendors or placing orders for souvenirs.

In this chapter you'll find information to help you maintain records, show you what type of information to collect (and why), give you examples of how the information you collect can be used, demonstrate how to organize information in the most efficient, time-saving or space-saving way, show how to prevent duplicating effort and give you ways to organize or lay out the information for easy use.

Looking for a business to help you with your reunion plans?

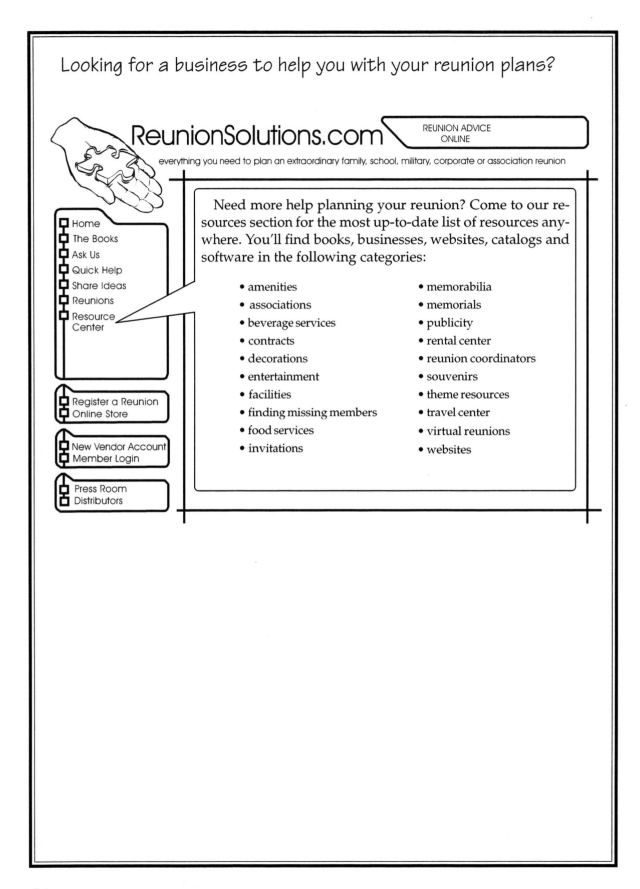

ReunionSolutions.com

REUNION ADVICE ONLINE

everything you need to plan an extraordinary family, school, military, corporate or association reunion

- Home
- The Books
- Ask Us
- Quick Help
- Share Ideas
- Reunions
- Resource Center

- Register a Reunion
- Online Store

- New Vendor Account
- Member Login

- Press Room
- Distributors

Need more help planning your reunion? Come to our resources section for the most up-to-date list of resources anywhere. You'll find books, businesses, websites, catalogs and software in the following categories:

- amenities
- associations
- beverage services
- contracts
- decorations
- entertainment
- facilities
- finding missing members
- food services
- invitations

- memorabilia
- memorials
- publicity
- rental center
- reunion coordinators
- souvenirs
- theme resources
- travel center
- virtual reunions
- websites

Member Data Sheet

Name: First _____ Middle: _____ Last _____ Married _____

Address _____
City _____ St ____ Zip ____
Phone _____ Fax _____
E-mail _____
URL _____
Address valid on: _____

Address _____
City _____ St ____ Zip ____
Phone _____ Fax _____
E-mail _____
URL _____
Address valid on: _____

Address _____
City _____ St ____ Zip ____
Phone _____ Fax _____
E-mail _____
URL _____
Address valid on: _____

Address _____
City _____ St ____ Zip ____
Phone _____ Fax _____
E-mail _____
URL _____
Address valid on: _____

Birthdate _____
Spouse _____
Children _____
Parents _____
Siblings _____
Friends _____
Schools Attended _____
Degrees Earned _____
Profession _____
Employer _____
Military Service _____
Memberships _____
Hobbies _____

Miscellaneous

State and Local Government Sources
- Criminal/Civil Court Records
- Drivers' License and Motor Vehicle Registration
- Sporting Licenses
- Vital Statistics Records
- Voter Registration Records

School Sources
- High School records
- College Alumni Association

Professional Sources
- Board of Licenses
- Trade Union/Professional Assn Membership Directories
- Retired Civil Service Employees Directory

Library Sources
- Internet E-mail Search
- CD-ROM Phone Directories
- City Phone Books
- Nat'l Dir of Addr and Telephone Numbers
- City Directories
- Newspaper Files
- Obituary Files
- USGPO Directory
- Who's Who
- Business Guide to Corporate Executives
- Local Newspaper

Internet Resources
- www.classmates.com
- www.whitepages.com
- www.nara.gov
- www.whowhere.com
- www.switchboard.com
- www.anywho.com
- www.military.com
- www.knowx.com
- www.genealogy.com
- www.555-1212.com

Military Sources
- Air Force Locator Service (Active)
- US Army Locator Service (Active)
- US Army Reserve Personnel Center
- US Coast Guard Locator Service (Active)
- US Marine Corps Personnel Center
- US Navy Personnel Service (Active)
- Nationwide Locator

- Air Force Retired Pay Division
- Army Retired Pay Division
- Coast Guard Retired Pay Division
- Marine Retired Pay Division
- Navy Retired Pay Division

Communications

Kickoff Communique sent (date): _____ Received back: _____

Volunteered to: _____ Reply Card sent: _____

Assigned to Chairperson: _____

Teaser sent (date): _____

Invitation sent (date): _____ Received back: _____

Reminder sent (date): _____ Received back: _____

Receipt for payment sent (date): _____

Payment Information

Full Package single	Number _____	Price _____	Paid _____
Full Package couple	Number _____	Price _____	Paid _____
A la carte item	Number _____	Price _____	Paid _____
A la carte item	Number _____	Price _____	Paid _____
A la carte item	Number _____	Price _____	Paid _____
A la carte item	Number _____	Price _____	Paid _____
A la carte item	Number _____	Price _____	Paid _____
A la carte item	Number _____	Price _____	Paid _____
TOTAL		Price _____	Paid _____
Check Number _____			

Chapter 11

Lost and Found:
Locating Your Missing Members

or many reunions, the biggest single job may be locating the guests. If you have a large number to locate or if considerable time has passed since they've been contacted, the sooner you start the search, the better. No matter how big the challenge seems, take heart, there are numerous ways you can track people down.

Because your member search will have a direct impact on your attendance, it's important to consider the impact your member search will have on your reunion overall. How much time, effort and money you'll expend on your member search depends upon whether you'll go to the ends of the earth to find every member, whether you'll expect members to take the initiative to find you or something in between.

A common complaint about reunions comes from people who show up on a missing list, when no *apparent* effort was made to find them. Don't leave your guests with the impression that you aren't interested in having *everyone* attend.

The key to an effective member search is to search the places where you're likely to have the greatest successes *first*. By compiling as much information as you know about each member, you can narrow the missing list before you go on to each successive round.

In this chapter you'll find information about how your member search will affect your attendance, help to identify the challenges a member search presents and tips to help find your missing members.

Want to see examples of the ideas we've discussed in this book?

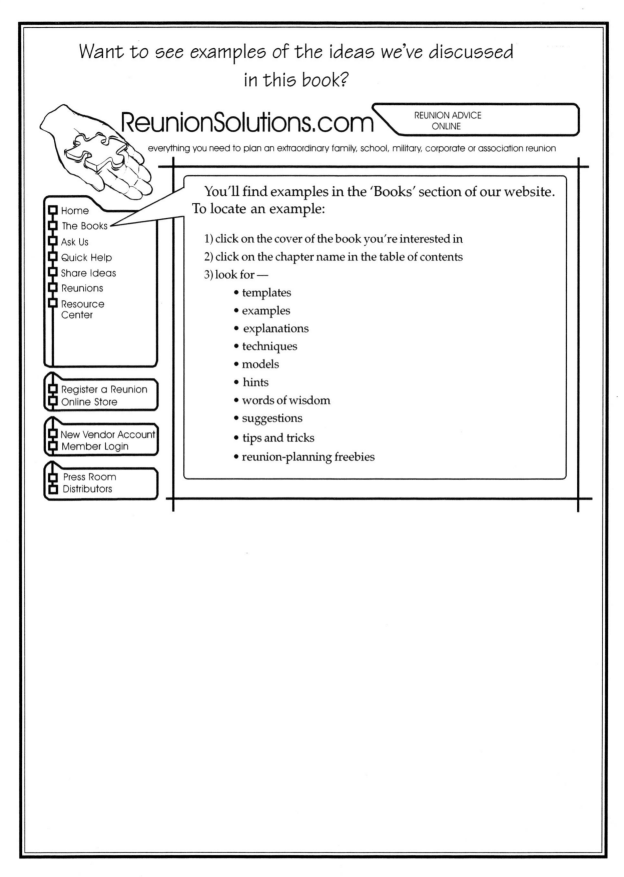

ReunionSolutions.com

REUNION ADVICE ONLINE

everything you need to plan an extraordinary family, school, military, corporate or association reunion

- Home
- The Books
- Ask Us
- Quick Help
- Share Ideas
- Reunions
- Resource Center

- Register a Reunion
- Online Store

- New Vendor Account
- Member Login

- Press Room
- Distributors

You'll find examples in the 'Books' section of our website. To locate an example:

1) click on the cover of the book you're interested in

2) click on the chapter name in the table of contents

3) look for —
- templates
- examples
- explanations
- techniques
- models
- hints
- words of wisdom
- suggestions
- tips and tricks
- reunion-planning freebies

Search Methods Checklist

Search Method	Location	Search Cost

Search Methods Checkoff Sheet

State and Local Government Sources

- [ ] Voter Registration Records
- [ ] Drivers' License and Motor Vehicle Registration
- [ ] Criminal/Civil Court Records
- [ ] Vital Statistics Records
- [ ] Sporting Licenses

Library Sources

- [ ] Internet E-mail Search
- [ ] CD-ROM Phone Directories
- [ ] City Phone Books
- [ ] National Directory of Addr and Telephone Numbers
- [ ] City Directories
- [ ] Newspaper Files
- [ ] Obituary Files
- [ ] USGPO Directory
- [ ] Who's Who
- [ ] Business Guide to Corporate Executives
- [ ] Local Newspaper

Internet Resources

- [ ] www.classmates.com
- [ ] www.nara.gov
- [ ] www.switchboard.com
- [ ] www.military.com
- [ ] www.genealogy.com
- [ ] www.whitepages.com
- [ ] www.whowhere.com
- [ ] www.anywho.com
- [ ] www.knowx.com
- [ ] www.555-1212.com

School Sources

- [ ] High School records
- [ ] College Alumni Association

Professional Sources

- [ ] Board of Licenses
- [ ] Trade Union/Professional Association Membership Directories
- [ ] Retired Civil Service Employees Directory

Military Sources

- [ ] Air Force Locator Service (Active)
- [ ] US Army Locator Service (Active)
- [ ] US Army Reserve Personnel Center
- [ ] US Coast Guard Locator Service (Active)
- [ ] US Marine Corps Personnel Center
- [ ] US Navy Personnel Service (Active)
- [ ] Nationwide Locator
- [ ] Air Force Retired Pay Division
- [ ] Army Retired Pay Division
- [ ] Coast Guard Retired Pay Division
- [ ] Marine Retired Pay Division
- [ ] Navy Retired Pay Division

Volunteer Assignment Sheet

Volunteer	
Search method assigned	
Deadline	
Results	
Volunteer	
Search method assigned	
Deadline	
Results	
Volunteer	
Search method assigned	
Deadline	
Results	
Volunteer	
Search method assigned	
Deadline	
Results	
Volunteer	
Search method assigned	
Deadline	
Results	
Volunteer	
Search method assigned	
Deadline	
Results	
Volunteer	
Search method assigned	
Deadline	
Results	
Volunteer	
Search method assigned	
Deadline	
Results	
Volunteer	
Search method assigned	
Deadline	
Results	
Volunteer	
Search method assigned	
Deadline	
Results	
Volunteer	
Search method assigned	
Deadline	
Results	

Telephone Contact Script

Hello, this is _____(your name)_____ from ___(name of your organization or your reunion)___

We're in the initial stages of planning our reunion and we don't have a current address for _____(name of the missing person)_____. Could you help me out with this?

If you reach a member directly, be sure to pass along all information available about the reunion. You might as well plant the seed about attending the reunion as early as you can. Then thank the person for updating their information and let them know when you plan to send out more detailed information or an invitation.

If the person you are calling doesn't have your member's current address information, ask for a spouse's name, married name, children's names, close friends or associates — other information that could lead you to the person you seek.

- Would you happen to know ...
- Are you in contact with someone else who would know ...

If the person you are calling is reluctant to give you information, offer them your name, address and telephone number and request that they pass it along to the person you're inquiring about.

- I don't blame you for being cautious ...
- How about if I send information to you that you could pass along ...

If you reach a person with the same name who is not a member of your group, apologize for the inconvenience and assure them that you will have their address and phone number removed from your list.

- I apologize. We must have gotten your information by mistake. I'll be sure to take your number off our list.

If you reach someone who is angry, apologize for the interruption and assure them that you will have their number removed from your list. Even if the person you have reached is a part of your group, if they don't want to be contacted, honor that feeling.

- I apologize for interrupting. I'll be sure to take your name off our list.

Have basic information about the reunion ready such as pricing, dates, times, places, souvenirs, website URL, a committee contact name and phone number or e-mail.

If the person indicates that the person you seek has died, give your condolences.

- I'm so sorry for your loss ...
- I'm so sorry to hear that. When did he/she pass away?

If you're planning to honor deceased members during the reunion, ask if the family member would like to participate in the memorials. Suggest that they contribute photographs, stories, anything that will spark memories. Use your judgment when asking for details of the death. If you get a death date, you will be able to search for an obituary for use in the Reunion Book or at the reunion.

- We're planning a_____ in honor of our deceased.
Would you like to contribute photographs, a memorial page, or an obituary?

When you're at an end, thank the person for the information you have received.

- Thanks so much for your time and the information you have provided on_____
It's important to our reunion plans to be able to give all of our old (friends, classmates or shipmates) a chance to attend.

Investigator Interview Checklist

Company Name:		
Address:		
Contact Name:	Phone:	Fax:
E-mail:	URL:	

Investigator's experience

Specialty _____

Professional association memberships _____

Investigator's license

Size of your list

Search methods suggested	Off-limits search methods

Fees

Hourly rate_____ Per-diem/travel_____

Fee per-find _____ Fee if no-find _____

Success rate

Information Return

Deadlines

Current client list/references

Billing Data

Deposit date _____ Deposit amount_____

Deposit date _____ Deposit amount_____

Final payment due _____ Final payment amount_____

Payment methods accepted _____

Signing a Contract with an Investigator

Consider the following before you fill out an order form or negotiate a contract with an investigator:

Precise description of service or product

- search methods which are acceptable and which are not
- what is considered a dead end
- how many investigators will be working with you
- what form the list will be delivered to you — database file, ASCII delimited file, word-processing file, etc.
- which computer databases will be searched

Dates, places, times

- date of the reunion
- meeting times and places with the investigator
- when the search will be completed
- final list of finds due before the invitation goes out

Contact person

- the name and phone number of the contact person for the firm
- the name and phone number of the investigator who will be working with you directly
- get an after hours or emergency number

Charges, fees, and deposits

- fee per search or fee per find
- whether there will be a charge if there are no finds
- hourly rate
- any discounts that apply

Methods of payment accepted

- cash, personal or committee check, credit card, billing on account, money order

Payment schedule

- when deposits are due
- when installments or final payment is due
- interest (if charged)
- when deposit is returned if not applied to the final bill

Not to exceed clause

- per-person charges not to exceed a certain amount
- total charges not to exceed

Extra charges

- copying
- computer charges
- phone charges
- travel or per diem expenses

Cancellation Policy

- no penalties if you cancel before a specified date
- if you cancel, payment of actual expenses incurred only
- if they cancel, payment of expenses incurred in finding another investigator

Deliveries or pickup

- who is responsible for delivery or pickup of the final list

Shipping method

- if the information is to be shipped to you, by which method — USPS, UPS, registered, insured, overnight, FTP, e-mail, or download

Staff's responsibilities

- when and how the investigator will contact you with information and updates
- how the information will be given to the committee

Committee's responsibilities

- what information you will provide to the private investigator in order to get started
- who has the authority to expand the investigator's search

Non-Performance Penalty

- if the investigator does not complete your search by the required deadline and you have to pay someone else more to do a rush job, the investigator should pay any rush fees you'll be charged
- if the investigator uses a search method you prohibited, there should be a reduction in price
- if more than 10% of the addresses you've been given come back as bad addresses, then there should be a reduction in the bill

Chapter 12

The Law of the Land: Contracts

contract is nothing more than a voluntary promise between two parties — an exchange of services for money, an exchange of products for money or an exchange of services for services. Whether you realize it or not, you enter into contracts every day. Every time you purchase something at a store, use your credit card or accept an order form with a description of services, you're operating under the terms of a contract. You enter into contracts every day. In most cases, the terms for both parties are clear and the contract is fulfilled to both parties' expectations. The more specific you are about what you're paying for, the less likely a misunderstanding will leave you or your reunion guests disappointed.

Unfortunately, the very word *contract* conjures up fear in the hearts of most ordinary humans. Take heart — nowhere is it written that you have to be a lawyer to enter into or write a good contract. Contracts don't have to be long and complicated, they don't all have fine print, they're not all written in archaic English and no term in a contract is written in stone.

There are five elements that must exist to constitute a contract: an offer, consideration, acceptance, party eligibility and the subject of the contract must be legal. Once the five elements exist ... you have a contract.

In this chapter you'll find information about the basics of contracts, answers to some common questions about contracts and a discussion about copyrights.

Things to Watch for in a Contract

An Offer
- a proposal to exchange one thing for another

An Acceptance
- a voluntary acceptance of the offer

Consideration
- an exchange of something of value for something else of value

Eligible Parties
- contracts must be entered into by competent adults

Legal Purpose
- the subject contracted for must be legal

Include the following in your reunion contracts

- ☐ A precise description of the service or product
- ☐ All dates, places and times
- ☐ The name and phone number of the contact person
- ☐ All charges, fees and deposits
- ☐ Methods of payment accepted
- ☐ The payment schedule
- ☐ A not to exceed clause if there are any open-ended charges
- ☐ A cancellation policy
- ☐ All deadlines or due dates
- ☐ Responsibility for pickup or delivery
- ☐ The shipping method to be used
- ☐ Staffing and equipment requirements
- ☐ The vendor's responsibilities
- ☐ The committee's responsibilities
- ☐ A penalty for non-performance
- ☐ Copyright policy

Chapter 13

You are Cordially Invited:
Invitations and other Communications

From the time you begin planning to the day of the reunion, you'll need to communicate with your members. You may need communications to encourage committee membership, to announce that reunion plans are under way, to send out details of the reunion events and, most importantly, communications to invite members to attend.

Your communications are the ambassadors for the reunion. They're your marketing tools. They embody everything you've planned — every statement, every graphic or photograph, even the layout and typestyle will leave an impression with your reader. Your message should be consistent, reflect the style of the reunion and persuasive enough to get your members to act. The number of communications needed differs from reunion to reunion, although *all* reunions need some type of invitation. If your reunion is small, your members are very close or you hold an annual reunion, you may not need to send more than just a simple invitation and a request to RSVP. But larger reunions, especially if you're planning a complex, elaborate or more expensive reunion, may need to put more effort into marketing. By marketing we mean convincing group members that the money they'll spend to attend the reunion will be well worth it. There are many ways to communicate with your members — postal or electronic mail, electronic greeting cards, the telephone and the internet. *Use them all!*

In this chapter you'll find information to help you get more mileage from your communication efforts by writing an effective message, designing communications to get noticed or hiring a professional designer to help.

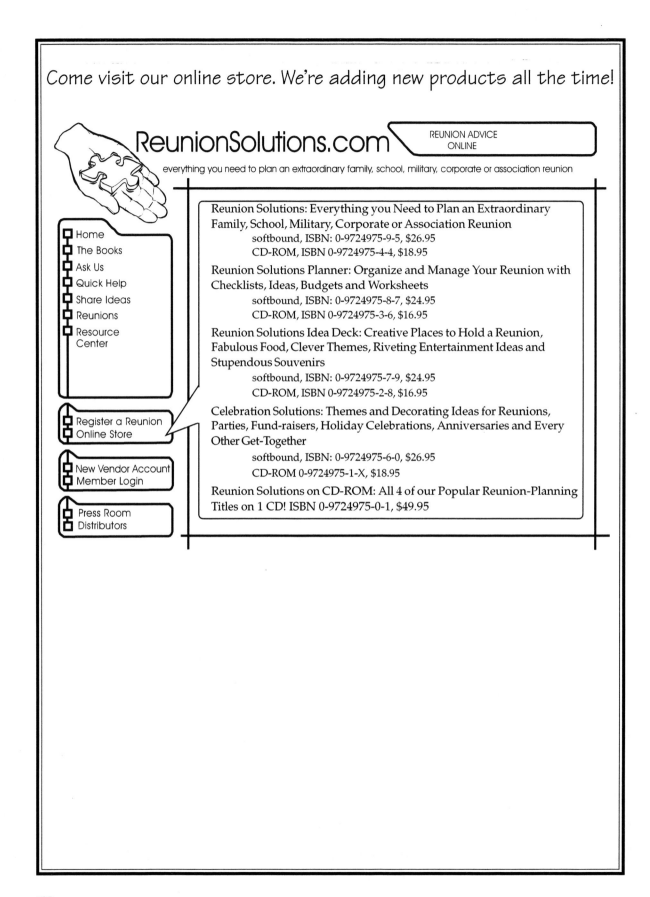

Come visit our online store. We're adding new products all the time!

ReunionSolutions.com

REUNION ADVICE
ONLINE

everything you need to plan an extraordinary family, school, military, corporate or association reunion

Home
The Books
Ask Us
Quick Help
Share Ideas
Reunions
Resource Center

Register a Reunion
Online Store

New Vendor Account
Member Login

Press Room
Distributors

Reunion Solutions: Everything you Need to Plan an Extraordinary Family, School, Military, Corporate or Association Reunion
softbound, ISBN: 0-9724975-9-5, $26.95
CD-ROM, ISBN 0-9724975-4-4, $18.95

Reunion Solutions Planner: Organize and Manage Your Reunion with Checklists, Ideas, Budgets and Worksheets
softbound, ISBN: 0-9724975-8-7, $24.95
CD-ROM, ISBN 0-9724975-3-6, $16.95

Reunion Solutions Idea Deck: Creative Places to Hold a Reunion, Fabulous Food, Clever Themes, Riveting Entertainment Ideas and Stupendous Souvenirs
softbound, ISBN: 0-9724975-7-9, $24.95
CD-ROM, ISBN 0-9724975-2-8, $16.95

Celebration Solutions: Themes and Decorating Ideas for Reunions, Parties, Fund-raisers, Holiday Celebrations, Anniversaries and Every Other Get-Together
softbound, ISBN: 0-9724975-6-0, $26.95
CD-ROM 0-9724975-1-X, $18.95

Reunion Solutions on CD-ROM: All 4 of our Popular Reunion-Planning Titles on 1 CD! ISBN 0-9724975-0-1, $49.95

Communications Plan Checklist

Common Elements

- [ ] Confirm the contact information of the recipient
- [ ] Missing list
- [ ] Member Locator Return Form
- [ ] Committee contact information
- [ ] Message to get the recipient's attention
- [ ] Make it easy to respond
- [ ] Website URL
- [ ] Action you want the reader to take

Communication Description

What's the message of this communication?

What are we trying to achieve with this communication?

Who should receive this communication?

When should we send this communication?

What action do we want the reader to take?

What should we expect back?

What will we do with what we get back from this communication?

Mailing Components Checklist

Invitation

- [ ] Date out _____
- [ ] Keep/Return symbol
- [ ] Envelope
- [ ] Reservation Order Form
- [ ] Reunion Book Information Sheet
- [ ] Reunion Book Explanation Sheet
- [ ] In Memory Sheet
- [ ] Trivia Sheet
- [ ] Missing List
- [ ] Maps
- [ ] General Information Sheet
- [ ] We Need Sheet
- [ ] Oops Postcard
- [ ] Wrap Up Sheet
- [ ] Encouragement to attend
- [ ] Return envelope
- [ ] Deadline to respond
- [ ] Mailing label
- [ ] Postage

Kickoff Communique

- [ ] Date out _____
- [ ] Committee Positions Form
- [ ] Member Locator Return Form
- [ ] Missing List

Teaser

- [ ] Date out _____
- [ ] Member Locator Return Form
- [ ] Missing List

Reminder Mailing

- [ ] Date out _____
- [ ] Deadline for response

Invitation for Special Guests

- [ ] Date out _____
- [ ] Deadline for response
- [ ] Special pricing

Volunteer Follow Up

- [ ] Assignment
- [ ] Assigned to
- [ ] When needed

Receipt for Registration

- [ ] Amount owed/paid
- [ ] Thank you

Graphic Designer Interview Checklist

Company Name:			
Address:			
Contact Name:		Phone:	Fax:
E-mail:		URL:	

Designer's experience

Professional association memberships _____

Copywriting _____ Graphics _____

Order Forms/Direct Mail_____

Designer's portfolio	**What the designer needs from you**

Designer's fees

Hourly rate_____ Per-piece rate _____

Design_____ Re-design_____

Reprints_____ Enlargements_____ Reductions_____ Digital copies_____

Additional services

Printer bids_____

Mailing houses_____

Copyrights

Deadlines

Current clients/references

Billing Data

Deposit date _____ Deposit amount_____

Deposit date _____ Deposit amount_____

Final payment due _____ Final payment amount_____

Payment methods accepted _____

Signing a Contract with a Graphic Designer

Consider the following before you fill out an order form or negotiate a contract with a design firm:

Precise description of service
- how many designs will you have to choose from (variations on one design or all originals) and in what form (electronic pre-press or camera-ready)
- whether copyrights will be assigned to you
- whether camera-ready preparation will be done
- whether printing or mailing services will be included

Dates, places, times
- date for each mailing to go out
- meeting dates, times and places

Contact person
- contact person and phone number for the firm
- name and phone number of the designer who will be doing your artwork
- get an after hours or emergency number

Charges, fees, and deposits
- fees for each service listed separately
- charges for initial design and redesign work
- hourly rate or project bid
- any discounts that apply

Methods of payment accepted
- cash, personal or committee check, credit card, billing on account, money order

Payment schedule
- when deposits are due
- payment in installments
- when final payment is due
- interest (if charged)
- when deposit is returned if not applied to the final bill

Not to exceed clause
- if your designer charges hourly, then put a limit on the total amount of time that can be spent upon the design

Extra charges
- whether production of camera-ready copy or electronic files will be charged extra
- whether screens, reductions or enlargements will be charged extra

Cancellation policy
- if you cancel, payment of actual expenses incurred only
- no penalties if you cancel before a specified date
- if the designer cancels, payment of expenses incurred in finding another designer and any rush fees that you might incur

Deadlines or due dates
- when designs will be ready for review and when final designs will finished
- design approval date
- redesign due
- final designs finished

Deliveries or pickup
- whether the artwork will be delivered or picked up by a member of the committee

Shipping method
- If the design work is to be shipped to you, by which method — USPS, UPS, registered, insured, overnight

Staffing or Equipment to be Used
- specify equipment for design (computer, hand drawn)
- specify your artist

Staff's responsibilities
- how many designs are expected
- how much variety in each design
- whether the staff artist will be responsible for original artwork or whether they will make an adaptation of a school mascot, family crest, etc.
- whether the designer has an established relationship with a printer and will get bids on printing services

Committee's responsibilities
- whether the committee will be responsible for providing copies of school mascots, mottos, troop insignias, logos, etc.
- who has the authority to approve designs

Non-Performance Penalty
- if design work is not completed in time for the printer to get the job done, the designer should pick up the extra cost of a rush job

Invitation Printer Interview Checklist

Company Name:	
Address:	
Contact Name:	Phone: Fax:
E-mail:	URL:

Printer's Process

Printer's portfolio

Printer's fees

Turnaround time

Paper in stock

Overage policy

Special Services

Labeling _____	Copywriting _____
Mailing_____	Typesetting_____
Envelope stuffing_____	Pasteup_____
Folding_____	Screens_____
Scans_____	Collating_____
Graphic design_____	Photography_____

Billing Data

Deposit date _____	Deposit amount_____
Deposit date _____	Deposit amount_____
Final payment due _____	Final payment amount_____
Payment methods accepted _____	

Signing a Contract with a Printer

Consider the following before you fill out an order form or negotiate a contract with a printer:

Precise description of service or product
- how many pieces will be produced
- what printing method will be used
- what paper and which ink will be used
- whether you will provide camera-ready art or the printer will produce it for you
- whether the mailing will be folded
- whether artwork or screens will be included
- whether the mailing will be sent directly to guests

Dates, places, times
- meeting dates, times and places

Contact person
- contact person and phone number for the company

Charges, fees, and deposits
- all charges for layout, typesetting, screens, printing, folding, collating, mailing
- whether there are discounts for volume
- any other discounts that apply

Methods of payment accepted
- personal or committee checks, billing on account, credit cards, money order, cash

Payment schedule
- when deposits are due
- payments in installments
- when final payment is due
- interest (if charged)
- when deposit is returned if not applied to the final bill

Not to exceed clause
- the percentage or dollar amount not to be exceeded for overages

Extra charges
- whether there are extra charges for collating, folding, and mailing, or whether these services are included in the printing price
- whether reductions, enlargements or screens are extra
- whether there's an extra charge for converting electronic files or for using electronic output

Cancellation policy
- no penalties if you cancel before a specified date
- if you cancel, payment of actual expenses incurred only
- if the printer cancels, payment of expenses incurred in finding another printer and paying for rush fees

Deadlines or due dates
- when originals are due to the printer
- when printed materials are due to be picked up or delivered

Deliveries or pickup
- whether the committee will be responsible for pickup or whether the printer will ship the materials to the committee or mail directly to the guest list

Shipping method
- If printing is to be shipped to you, indicate by which method — USPS, UPS, registered, insured, overnight

Staffing or Equipment to be Used
- whether the printing will be copied, offset printed, lithograph printed, color copied, 4-color printed, etc

Staff's irresponsibilities
- to spot check the work as it progresses for clean copies
- any layout or artwork that is to be done

Committee's responsibilities
- when wordprocessing and camera-ready artwork will be delivered to the printer
- whether the committee will proof the typesetting before printing

Non-Performance penalty
- if a wrong paper or ink color is used, the printer should make the job right without any cost to the committee

Chapter 14

Attention Getters:
Publicity

Before you write your promotional message, determine the one *key point* you want to get across and make sure you state it strongly and early on. What is it you want the reader, listener or viewer to know?

Knowing your audience is essential to choosing the promotional method most likely to be seen or heard by the right people. Taking a scattershot, throw-it-out-there approach isn't usually effective and an inefficient use of your resources. Targeting your publicity to a specific audience will make your publicity much more effective than an appeal to just anyone who might happen to see or hear your message. You're trying to reach members of a specific group, so before you can choose where to publicize, you've got to ask yourself — who's going to hear the message? Put yourself in the shoes of the person who will be reading, seeing or hearing your message. Which magazines or newspapers do members of your audience read? What radio stations do they listen to or television programs do they watch? Once you can answer these questions, you'll be able to design your publicity to reach your audience, using the media most likely to be seen, read of heard by these people. Before choosing a promotional method, ask yourself — will the specific audience you're trying to reach be visiting *this* website or reading *this* newspaper or listening to *this* radio station?

In this chapter you'll find information to help you identify your audience (who you're appealing to with your publicity), to choose the most appropriate place to generate publicity (the right method to reach the right audience) and then to come up with the right words to get your message across, in the most effective way possible.

PR Kit Checklist

☐ Stamped invitation packets

☐ Reminder card with contact name and phone number to get additional stamped invitation packets

☐ Inquiry log

☐ Fact sheet

Fact Sheet Contents
☐ Contact name
☐ Contact phone number
☐ Website address
☐ Reunion dates
☐ Event locations
☐ Start and end time for each event
☐ Cost
☐ Deadlines
☐ Souvenirs available

Publicity Methods Checklist

Publicity method	
Content	
Sent to	
Action taken	Example kept

Publicity method	
Content	
Sent to	
Action taken	Example kept

Publicity method	
Content	
Sent to	
Action taken	Example kept

Publicity method	
Content	
Sent to	
Action taken	Example kept

Publicity method	
Content	
Sent to	
Action taken	Example kept

Publicity method	
Content	
Sent to	
Action taken	Example kept

Publicity method	
Content	
Sent to	
Action taken	Example kept

Publicity method	
Content	
Sent to	
Action taken	Example kept

Practice Newsrelease

Contact Name: _____ For release: _____

Contact Phone Number:_____

Contact Address:_____

_____

Type of Publication

Publication's Audience

Your Audience

Essence of the Message

Headline

Who, When, Where, Why, What, How

Further details

Practice Query for Feature Articles

Editor's Name: _____

Editor's Title: _____

Editor's Address: _____

_____

Type of Publication

Publication's Audience

Your Audience

What makes your story unique

Proposed Headline

Who, When, Where, Why, What, How

Further details

Practice Poster (Leaflet)

Headline

Eye-catching graphic

Who, What, When, Where, Why, How

Details

Contact information

Publicist Interview Checklist

Company Name:

Address:

Contact Name: Phone: Fax:

E-mail: URL:

Publicist assigned to you

Publicist's experience

Professional association memberships _____

Publicist's portfolio

Media _____

Promotional methods _____

Copywriting _____

Fees

By campaign _____ By method _____

Research _____ By delivery _____

Message Approval

Special services

Copies of each publicity piece _____

Deadlines

Current client list/references

Billing Data

     Deposit date _____ Deposit amount _____

     Deposit date _____ Deposit amount _____

     Final payment due _____ Final payment amount _____

     Payment methods accepted _____

Signing a Contract with a Publicist

Consider the following before you negotiate a contract with a publicist or a public relations firm:

Precise description of service or product

- list of media and methods chosen
- whether the committee will have message approval before release
- Research appropriate media outlets for your group

Dates, places, times

- date of the reunion
- meeting dates, places, times

Contact person

- contact person and phone number for the firm
- name and phone number of the publicist who will be working with you directly
- get an after hours or emergency number

Charges, fees, and deposits

- whether you will be paying a flat fee, an hourly rate or a per -publicity piece charge
- retainer fee
- hourly rate
- any discounts that apply

Methods of payment accepted

- cash, personal or committee check, credit card, billing on account, money order

Payment schedule

- when deposits are due
- payments in installments
- when final payment is due
- interest (if charged)
- when deposit is returned if not applied to the final bill

Not to exceed clause

- per publicity piece or media type
- if there's an hourly charge, put a limit on the number of hours in the development phase. It's better to spend your money on the actual publicity

Extra charges

- printing or postage
- database search fees
- purchase of mailing lists

Cancellation Policy

- no penalties if you cancel before a specified date
- if you cancel, payment of actual expenses incurred only
- if they cancel, payment of expenses incurred in finding another investigator

Deadlines or due dates

- when information will be released to the media
- placement dates in which media

Deliveries or pickup

- who is responsible for delivery or pickup of the publicity pieces for your approval
- who is responsible for delivery of the publicity pieces to go out to the media

Shipping method

- when publicity is delivered to the media, by which method — USPS, UPS, registered, insured, overnight, fax, online, e-mail

Staffing or equipment to be used

- which media will be used
- what message will be sent to which media

Staff's irresponsibilities

- who will be responsible for contacting the media
- who will be writing the copy for PSAs and newsreleases
- provide copies of all articles generated to the committee
- provide copies of any TV or radio interviews that were aired

Committee's responsibilities

- what information, written or graphic materials will be provided by the committee
- who has the authority to extend the publicist's responsibilities

Non-performance penalty

- if the publicist does not complete your publicity materials by the required deadline and you have to pay someone else more to do a rush job the publicist should pay for the extra cost
- if the publicist doesn't use the media you have agreed upon, then there should be a reduction in the bill
- if the publicist doesn't reach the number of media contacts agreed upon, then there should be a reduction in the bill

Chapter 15

A World Wide Wonder:
Creating a Reunion Website

Websites are incredible tools for reunions. They can help you get the word out, allow members of your group to reconnect even before they meet at the reunion, give your members a way to contact the committee and help pass along information to your members. Websites aren't just about putting up pretty pages or fancy graphics, they're about providing information.

Your home page is like a storefront. Viewers should be able to tell from this first page what the site's about, who's behind the site, and what's available on the site. It's important to present that information at a glance and not force viewers to scroll and scroll and scroll to see what's available or find your navigation buttons. Section headings that make up your essential navigation should be visible on the opening screen. Fast loading graphics, information about what's available on the site, and a balanced, overall pleasing look are the best combination for a good home page.

Navigation is the most essential part of a website. Navigation allows the viewer to move from place to place within the site. If navigation is good, it tells the viewers where to begin and where it's possible to go. You can have all the cool graphics in the world, but if viewers can't figure out how to get from one place to the other, your information will never be found.

Most people can put together a simple website — and if you can't, a teenager you know probably can!

Site Map Storyboard

Homepage

Web Page Design Basics Checklist

Navigation Design

- [ ] Site map
- [ ] Common elements on every page
- [ ] Text links that look like links
- [ ] Buttons that look like buttons

Software

- [ ] HTML/Web Development
- [ ] Image editing
- [ ] Audio/Video editing
- [ ] Animation

Page Design

- [ ] Home page
- [ ] Pages not too busy
- [ ] Design for a horizontal screen
- [ ] Consistent design style
- [ ] Type big enough to read
- [ ] Consistent alignment
- [ ] Web-safe palette colors
- [ ] Logo top left
- [ ] Minimize download time
- [ ] Design within the usable area
- [ ] Consistent type styles
- [ ] Use fancy type sparingly
- [ ] Correct proximity
- [ ] Non-busy backgrounds

Designing to be Found

- [ ] Domain name
- [ ] Meta-tags
- [ ] Alt=IMG tags
- [ ] Page titles
- [ ] Keywords
- [ ] Search engines

Testing

- [ ] User testing

Security

- [ ] Password-protected personal info

Designing to be Used

- [ ] Keep it fresh

Search Engine Resources

Search Engine Tips

Search Engine Watch	www.searchenginewatch.com
Front Page Collection of Search Engines	www.thefrontpage.com/search/
Internet Search Almanac	www.vassiliansdepot.com/almaweb.html
Search Engine Placement Pointers	www.infoscavenger.com/engine.htm
Search Engine Secrets	www.globalserve.net/~iwb/search/index.html
Web Ranking Tools	www.bruceclay.com/web_rank.htm

Search Engines

Alta Vista	www.altavista.com
AOL Netfind	www.aol.com/netfind/
BizWeb	www.bizweb.com
Excite	www.excite.com
Hot Bot	www.hotbot.com
InfoSeek	www.infoseek.com
Linkcentre Directory	linkcentre.com
Lycos	www.lycos.com
MetaSearcher (name)	www.go2net.com
Overture (formerly GoTo)	www.overture.com
Small Business Directory	www.bizoffice.com
Trade Wave Galaxy	www.galaxy.com
WebCrawler	www.webcrawler.com
What-U-Seek	whatyouseek.com
Yahoo!	www.yahoo.com

Web Designer Interview Checklist

Company Name:		
Address:		
Contact Name:	Phone:	Fax:
E-mail:	URL:	

Designer's experience

Professional association memberships _____

Site URL _____

Site URL _____

Site URL _____

Design fees

Initial design_____ Redesign_____

Graphics creation_____ Scans_____

Site features

Design software_____

Approval process_____

Maintenance _____

Special Services

Relationships with ISPs_____

Relationships with Cyber-PR Agents_____

Deadlines

Client list/references

Billing Data

Deposit date _____ Deposit amount_____

Deposit date _____ Deposit amount_____

Final payment due _____ Final payment amount_____

Payment methods accepted_____

Signing a Contract with a Website Designer

Consider the following before you fill out an order form or negotiate a contract with a web designer:

Precise description of service or product

- exactly what the site will include, how many sections, how many pages, how many images, etc.
- whether the web designer will create original graphics or use Clip Art
- which software the website will be developed with
- how the website will be maintained
- all troubleshooting (broken links, missing graphics, unacceptable pages) will be fixed without charge

Dates, places, times

- date of the reunion
- dates for each meeting with the web designer
- dates the initial web design will be completed
- date the approved web design will be posted to the web
- dates for each change to the website

Contact person

- contact person and telephone number for the web designer
- get an after hours or emergency number in case the site crashes

Charges, fees and deposits

- all charges for site design, scanning, graphics
- whether these charges are hourly or a flat fee
- whether a deposit is required

Methods of payment accepted

- cash, personal or committee check, credit card, billing on account, money order

Payment schedule

- when deposit is due
- when incremental and final payments are due
- when deposits will be returned if they are not applied to the final bill

Not to exceed clause

- if charges will be hourly, you might want to include a not to exceed clause for the site design

Extra charges

- any services not included in the web design fee
- charges for scanning or preparing photographs
- charges for creating original graphics
- charges for postings to forums, generating forms, establishing e-commerce
- charges for altering your electronic files

Cancellation Policy

- cancellation date before which there are no charges
- penalty if you cancel after the no-penalty date
- penalty if the web designer cancels after the no-penalty date

Deadlines or due dates

- when the initial site design will be ready for your approval
- when the developed site will be ready for your approval
- when the site will be posted to the web
- when changes will be posted to the web

Deliveries or pickup

- whether the committee will be responsible for reviewing the site at the designer's office or online. Whether the web designer will ship or deliver a printed version to the committee for approval

Shipping method

- USPS, UPS, overnight, registered, insured, FTP, download, e-mail

Software or Equipment to be Used

- if a specific web authorizing software is to be used to create the site so that the committee can maintain it, specify the software

Staff's responsibilities

- site and graphic design
- inclusion and development of visual images
- proofreading
- troubleshooting the site

Committee's responsibilities

- whether the committee will provide any electronic images to be used for the site
- to evaluate the site and give final approval before the site is posted to the web
- whether the committee will maintain the site after the initial design

Non-Performance Penalty

- if the website is not ready for posting by the agreed upon date, the designer should reduce the design fee
- if the designer misses scheduled updates, the designer should reduce the maintenance fee
- if the web designer cancels after the agreed upon cancellation date, the designer should have to pay for finding another web designer to do the job and any rush fees as a result
- if you cancel after the agreed upon date, you should limit yourself to actual work completed at that point

ISP Interview Checklist

Company Name:

Address:

Contact Name: Phone: Fax:

E-mail: URL:

ISP's experience

Reliability record _____

Package options

Webhosting _____

_____

Web access _____

_____

E-mail accounts _____

ISP's equipment

ISP's software support _____

Extra Services

Domain name registry _____
Infobots _____
Search engine submissions _____

Web designer recommendations

Client list/references

Billing Data

Deposit date _____ Deposit amount _____

Deposit date _____ Deposit amount _____

Final payment due _____ Final payment amount _____

Payment methods accepted _____

Signing a Contract with an Internet Service Provider

Consider the following before you fill out an order form or negotiate a contract with an ISP:

Precise description of service or product

- how much disk space and through traffic you'll be allowed
- whether you'll have FTP access to your site
- what software is supported and how the site will be maintained
- how many e-mail accounts will be included
- how you'll be able to monitor traffic to your site

Dates, places, times

- date the site will be posted
- dates for each meeting with the ISP

Contact person

- contact person and telephone number for the internet service provider
- get an after hours or emergency number in case the site crashes

Charges, fees and deposits

- all charges for monthly hosting fees, setup charges
- whether there are fees for traffic volume overages
- fees for e-mail accounts
- whether there are charges for FTP access
- whether a deposit is required

Methods of payment accepted

- cash, personal or committee check, credit card, billing on account, money order

Payment schedule

- when (if) deposit is due
- when monthly payments are due

Extra charges

- any services not included in the monthly hosting fees
- charges for traffic overage
- charges for additional e-mail accounts
- charges to register a domain name
- charges to submit site information to search engines

Cancellation Policy

- how many months the contract is in effect
- penalty if you cancel before the contract length date
- penalty if the ISP cancels your service causing you to find another ISP, including all setup and transfer fees with the new ISP

Deadlines or due dates

- when the site will be posted to the internet and (possibly) when the site will be removed from the internet

Deliveries or pickup

- if the ISP has software that needs to be installed, when the software will be delivered

Shipping method

- USPS, UPS, overnight, registered, insured, FTP, download

Staffing or Equipment to be Used

- what type of server your site will reside on
- secure server with encryption
- firewalls to prevent hackers from accessing the site

Staff's irresponsibilities

- site access reliability
- e-mail account access reliability
- DSL or dial-up connection reliability

Committee's responsibilities

- whether the committee will maintain the site
- to understand the ISPs policies on appropriate content and SPAM

Non-Performance Penalty

- if the site is not posted within a week or so of submission, the ISP should deduct a proportional amount of the monthly hosting fee
- if the site or e-mail access is inaccessible for significant periods or time, monthly hosting fees should be discounted accordingly

Cyber-PR Agent Interview Checklist

Company Name:

Address:

Contact Name: _____ Phone: _____ Fax: _____

E-mail: _____ URL: _____

Agent's experience

Professional association memberships _____

Media _____

Promotional methods _____

Copywriting _____

Agent's fees

Research _____
_____

Newsreleases _____
_____

Internet announcement sites _____
_____

Establishing links _____
_____

Newsgroups _____
_____

Client list/references

Billing Data

Deposit date _____ Deposit amount _____

Deposit date _____ Deposit amount _____

Final payment due _____ Final payment amount _____

Payment methods accepted _____

Signing a Contract with a Cyber-PR Agent

Consider the following before you fill out an order form or negotiate a contract with a cyber-PR agent:

Precise description of service or product
- what search engines your site will be submitted to
- which media contacts will receive e-mail newsreleases
- which newsgroups will receive postings
- which megasites will be queried for links
- which announcements sites will get a newsrelease

Dates, places, times
- date of the reunion
- dates for each meeting with the cyber-PR agent
- dates of the website launch
- date copy will be delivered to the cyber-PR agent
- dates of all information releases

Contact person
- contact person and telephone number for the cyber-PR agent
- get an after hours or emergency number in case of publicity snafus

Charges, fees and deposits
- all charges for writing and editing newsreleases
- all charges for researching potential media contacts
- all charges for search engine submissions
- all charges for sending newsreleases, newsgroup postings and other media contacts
- whether a deposit is required

Methods of payment accepted
- cash, personal or committee check, credit card, billing on account, money order

Payment schedule
- when deposit is due
- when incremental or final payment is due
- when deposits will be returned if they are not applied to the final bill

Not to exceed clause
- if there is an hourly charge for services, there should be a dollar amount not to be exceeded for the whole campaign

Extra charges
- any charges not included in the service fees
- charges for HTML or styled e-mail
- charges for copywriting or editing
- charges for hardcopy confirmation of search engine submissions
- charges for copies of newsreleases

Cancellation policy
- cancellation date before which there are no charges
- penalty if you cancel after the no-penalty date
- penalty if the cyber-PR agent cancels after the no-penalty date

Deadlines or due dates
- when newreleases will go out
- when search engine submissions will be made
- when newsgroup postings will be completed

Deliveries or pickup
- whether the committee or the cyber-PR agent will be responsible for delivering newreleases to the media

Shipping method
- USPS, UPS, overnight, registered, insured, download, FTP
- whether the cyber-PR agent can make drafts available on the web for committee approval

Staffing or Equipment to be Used
- if a specific search engine submission software will be used, specify it
- if stylized or HTML e-mail will be used

Staff's responsibilities
- proofreading copy submitted by the committee
- layout design for HTML or stylized e-mail
- research for appropriate submission and newsgroup sites
- follow-up with media contacts

Committee's responsibilities
- to have the reunion website up and running before search engine submissions
- to proofread and approve all copy before newsreleases are sent to the media
- provide all pertinent reunion information

Non-Performance Penalty
- if the newreleases or site submissions are delayed, the cyber-PR agent should be responsible for any rush or overnight delivery charges that might occur
- if the cyber-PR agent cancels after the agreed upon cancellation date, the cyber-PR agent should have to pay for finding another firm to do the job and any rush fees as a result
- if you cancel after the agreed upon date, limit yourself to actual expenses incurred to that point

Chapter 16

Location! Location!! Location!!!:
Finding a Facility

*N*egotiating with a facility will be one of the first things you'll do after you define your reunion. You may be looking for an outdoor facility with minimal amenities or an indoor facility with a wide range of services. You may be looking for a facility for a single event or multiple events. The most important thing is to choose a facility that's right for the atmosphere of the event. Make sure the event you're planning can actually *function* in the space you've chosen, so consider the style, space, catering, bar service, lighting, electricity, equipment, style, price, guest comfort and whether the facility can accommodate your guests with special needs such as the disabled or the elderly. Make certain it will be able to accommodate your plans for decorating, themes, food service and entertainment. Before you can make a choice, though, you've got to make a visit. Go to the facility to experience the atmosphere to envision how your event will work in the space.

So where *will* you hold your reunion? There are dozens of creative and clever places to hold a reunion. Some are tried and true, some are a little out of the ordinary — and that's our point. Any place can be a great place. It all depends upon your event idea. You can create an event around an unusual location or try something completely unexpected. There are some limits, though. Some people just will not go down into a cave or up into a hot air balloon — even for a great party!

In this chapter you'll find information to help you find the facility that will best suit the plans for your events and any over-night accommodations you may need.

Room Setup Styles

Scattered rounds

The scattered round table setup is by far the most common. Scattered rounds are used to put the maximum number of people in a minimal amount of space. Round tables seat anywhere from four to twelve and table sizes can be alternated to give the room a less uniform appearance. If you're going to use scattered rounds and have a presentation, make sure that all dining is finished before the presentation begins because at least one quarter of the audience will have to turn their chairs around in order to see the presentation.

Conference style

Conference style is good if you have a small group and you want everyone to be able to see and communicate with each other. *This style works best with small groups.*

U-shape

U-Shape is good for presentations because everyone is looking inward and toward the front and no one's view is obstructed. *(If guests will be seated on the inside of the U, allow plenty of space).*

Hollow square

Hollow square style is good if you want to put something on display in the middle of the tables. Sometimes a hollow square is given a small aisle to facilitate service. Guests can be seated within an almost hollow square as long as there is adequate space.

Classroom style

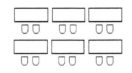

Classroom style easily accommodates a head table or presentations because guests will be able to see without having to turn their chairs around.

Chevron style

Chevron style is also good for presentations because tables are angled toward the center so that no one's view is blocked.

Reception style

Reception style is ideal if you are planning for cocktails and light hors d'oeuvres where most guests will be standing.

Table Sizing Chart

Table size	Seats/people	Table cloth size
72" round	10-12	132"
60" round	8-10	120"
54" round	6-8	114"
48" round	4-6	108"
36" round	4	96"

Indoor Facility Interview Checklist

Company Name:		
Address:		
Contact Name:	Phone:	Fax:
E-mail:	URL:	

Event Room

Date(s) available

Time available	Starting time	Ending time
Room rental fees	Deposit	Due by	Waived

Cancellation policy

Damage policy	Cleanup fees
Maximum occupancy	Options for add'l rooms

Room dimensions

Room fixtures/obstacles

Room features

Atmosphere	Thermostat control
Lighting	Lighting control
Dance floor	Electrical needs
Other equipment	Wall dividers

Tables	Square	Round	Oval	Rectangle	Condition

Room Setup	Scattered Rounds	Conference Style	U-Shape	Hollow Square
	Banquet Style	Classroom Style	Chevron Style	Reception Style

Table linens	Centerpieces		
Condition of the:	Chairs	Glassware	Silverware	China

Food service setup

Bar setup

Decoration space:	Floor	Walls	Ceiling	Free-standing

Decorating rules

Security	Locked equipment room	Coat/hat check

Handicap accessible

Parties in adjacent rooms	Contract negotiations
Construction plans	Union rules

Billing Data

Deposit date _____ Deposit amount_____

Deposit date _____ Deposit amount_____

Final payment due _____ Final payment amount_____

Payment methods accepted _____

Indoor Facility Interview Checklist

Amenities				
Guest rooms	Single	Double	Suite	Family
Group rates	Single	Double	Suite	Family
Guest room condition		Non-Smoking Rooms		Handicap Accessible
Hospitality suite				
Maps/brochures		Driving instructions		
Transportation: to airport		to train/bus	to sites	
Marquee		Cost	Message	
Sign frames		Sign stands		Glass sign cases
Concierge services		Doorman services		
Freight elevators				
Insurance		Liquor license		
Music license				
Recreation facilities		Cost	Hours	
Parking		Cost	Hours	
Valet Parking		Cost	Hours	
Cleaner		Cost	Hours	
Babysitting		Cost	Hours	
Restaurant		Price range	Hours	
Room Service		Price range	Hours	
Gift shop			Hours	
Check cashing		Fees	Hours	
ATMs				
Emergency facilities		Emergency number		

AV Equipment			
Sound System	Loudspeaker	TV	VCR
Monitor	Flip Chart	Podium	Microphones
Slide Projector	Movie Projector	Computer Projector	
Lighting effects	Laser shows	Robotic lights	

Security	Around the area		Within the facility
Parking			

Notes

Indoor Facility Room Sketch

Floor Plan

Proposed Room Layout

Signing a Contract with an Indoor Facility

Consider the following before you fill out an order form or negotiate a contract with an indoor facility:

Precise description of service or product
- banquet room name, size, setup arrangement
- food and bar service, menu, setup
- what the package price includes
- prices for all amenities, recreation and guest rooms
- room security

Dates, places, times
- date of the reunion
- start and end times of the event, setup and vacate times
- whether the room is available for rehearsals
- date that extra guest rooms must be released back to the hotel
- date to finalize numbers

Contact person
- name of the sales manager
- name of the person who will be in attendance the night of the reunion

Charges, fees, and deposits
- any fees not included in the package price
- all discounts or interest that apply

Methods of payment accepted
- cash, personal or committee check, credit card, billing on account, money order

Payment schedule
- when deposits and final payments are due
- when deposits will be returned if they are not used to cover damages or applied to the final bill

Not to exceed clause
- watch for any open-ended charges such as service or administrative fees

Extra charges
- liability insurance
- breakage/damage, cleanup or setup charges
- charges for changes to setup or service
- taxes, finance charges, security fees, gratuities
- charges for dance floors, special linens or china, centerpieces, piano, marquee postings, AV equipment
- charges for offsite transportation

Cancellation Policy
- no penalties if you cancel before a specified date
- if you cancel, payment of actual expenses incurred only or based upon profits lost, but not revenue lost
- if they cancel, payment of expenses incurred in finding another facility

Decoration Policy
- what can be used on walls, ceilings, floors, tables
- freestanding items
- lighting

Alcohol Policy
- who will and who won't be served alcohol
- how and whether IDs will be checked
- how intoxicated patrons will be treated
- transportation plan for intoxicated guests

Clean Up Policy
- responsibility for trash and decorations cleanup

Deliveries or pickup
- when the facility will be open for deliveries
- where deliveries will be held
- when the committee will have access to delivered objects or storage rooms

Shipping method
- If any information is to be shipped to you, by which method — USPS, UPS, registered, insured, overnight

Staffing or Equipment to be Used
- include a precise description of serving pieces, china, silverware, table cloths, centerpieces
- specify the number of servers per guest to fit the level of service that you require for both food and bar service

Staff's irresponsibilities
- what percent overage will be allowed in the menu
- how the staff will be dressed
- brochures or postcards of the facility for invitations or check-in packets, maps of the area
- floor plans with setups shown

Committee's responsibilities
- delivery date if reunion t-shirts or costumes for the staff to wear
- who will be available during each event to answer questions on behalf of the committee
- who has the authority to extend services

Non-Performance Penalty
- if the facility makes a room substitution because of other reservations or because of a change in your numbers, consider some kind of compensation such as additional decorations, better menu, free round of drinks, or an additional service
- if the facility does not have the room ready at your scheduled setup time, allow for an extended use of the room after your shutdown time
- if the menu or bar service was not what was agreed to, there should be a reduction in price

Outdoor Facility Interview Checklist

Company Name:	
Address:	
Contact Name:	Phone: Fax:
E-mail:	URL:

Atmosphere

Place to prepare food	
Access for caterer	Place for beverage service
Lighting	Electrical needs
Parking	Shade
Running water	Restrooms
Handicap accessible	Construction plans
Parties in adjacent areas	Inclement weather plans

Amenities

Campsites	Boating
Hiking	Biking
Nature walks	Ranger programs
Store	Signs
Concessions	Souvenirs
Guides	Outfitters

Shelter/Campsite

Date(s) available		Maximum occupancy
Time available	Starting time	Ending time
Cancellation policy	Damage policy	Cleanup fees
Shelter features		

Policies

Decorating rules
Alcohol policy
Cleanup policy
Smoking policy

Emergencies

Security	Access to phones
Access to first aid	Access to rangers/park personnel
Nearest emergency facility	Emergency personnel response time
Notes:	

Billing Data

Deposit date _____ Deposit amount_____

Deposit date _____ Deposit amount_____

Final payment due _____ Final payment amount_____

Payment methods accepted _____

Outdoor Facility Area Sketch

Area Map

Shelter/Facility Floor Plan

Signing a Contract for an Outdoor Facility

Consider the following before you fill out an order form or negotiate a contract with an outdoor facility:

Precise description of service or product
- whether there are on-site catering or concessionaires and prices
- whether there will be cooking facilities available
- all rules for bringing in food or alcohol
- whether a permit is required
- whether decorations are allowed

Dates, places, times
- date and location of the reunion
- start and end times of the event
- setup and vacate times

Contact person
- who is available on the day of the reunion
- get an after hours or emergency number

Charges, fees, and deposits
- charges for each service
- all discounts that apply
- any interest that will be charged

Methods of payment accepted
- cash, personal or committee check, credit card, billing on account, money order

Payment schedule
- when deposits are due
- when final payment is due
- when deposits will be returned if they are not used to cover damages or applied to the final bill

Not to exceed clause
- watch for any open-ended charges such as service or administrative fees

Extra charges
- fees for cleanup or damage
- taxes
- charges for electricity
- charges for ranger or rescue services
- parking, hiking or camping permit fees
- equipment rental fees

Cancellation Policy
- if you cancel, payment of actual expenses incurred only
- no penalties if you cancel before a specified date
- if they cancel, payment of expenses incurred in finding another facility

Decoration Policy
- what can be used on walls or ceilings of any structures
- what can be setup freestanding in the area

Alcohol Policy
- whether alcohol is allowed at the site
- who will and who won't be served alcohol
- how and whether IDs will be checked

Clean Up Policy
- who is responsible for trash and decorations pickup
- pack in, pack out rules

Deliveries or pickup
- when the facility will be open for deliveries

Shipping method
- If any information is to be shipped to you, by which method — USPS, UPS, registered, insured, overnight

Staffing or Equipment to be Used
- if there is to be a ranger or a guide for tours

Staff's responsibilities
- whether the staff or the committee is responsible for cleanup

Committee's responsibilities
- directional signs along roadways
- who will be available during each event to answer questions on behalf of the committee
- when contact information for guests will be delivered
- who has the authority to extend services

Non-Performance Penalty
- if the facility makes a substitution of locations because of other reservations, consider some kind of compensation such as an additional service or a reduction in price
- if the facility does not have the area ready at your scheduled setup time, allow for an extended use of the facility after your shutdown time

Tent Rental Checklist

- ☐ Tent size needed _____
- ☐ Pole tent
- ☐ Framed tent
- ☐ Anchored or set into the ground
- ☐ Flooring
- ☐ Lighting
- ☐ Seating
- ☐ Tables
- ☐ Heaters
- ☐ Adequate ventilation for cooking
- ☐ Sidewalls_____ Cloth_____ Clear_____ Netted _____
- ☐ Generators/electricity
- ☐ Sound system
- ☐ Permits
- ☐ Overnight security

Tent Space Sketch

Chapter 17

Menu Madness:
Selecting the Food

hat can we say about food? Everyone loves to eat! Go to a wedding reception — you eat. Go to an elegant party — you eat. Even most cocktail receptions offer something to munch on. For many reunions, food is a *major* consideration, not to mention that it may be the single biggest item in your budget.

What you serve and how you serve it should be in keeping with the style, feel and atmosphere of the *event* you're planning. It's disappointing to spoil an elegant setting with dry, rubber chicken. Likewise, it's frustrating to manage escargot forks at a windy picnic table.

Food is also an important measure of value for your guests. Most people know how much a nice restaurant meal will cost them, and that's what they'll use to evaluate whether what they've paid for the event was a good deal. The more you can do to sell the whole event as a package — the food, atmosphere, decorations and souvenirs — the more likely your guests will be satisfied. After all, it's hard to convince people that $50 per person is a good deal if they're eating dull, bland food. It's better to "wow 'em" a little bit.

In this chapter you'll find information to help you choose between food-service styles, to figure out an appropriate menu and figure out how much food to order or fix. Then, if you're going to hire a caterer, we'll give you some event planning wisdom that will make working with a caterer a pleasure.

Signing a Contract with a Caterer

Consider the following before you fill out an order form or negotiate a contract with a caterer:

Precise description of service or product
- precise menu and food service style
- percentage of overage prepared
- special meals
- contingency for walk-ins

Dates, places, times
- date of the reunion
- location of the reunion
- start and end times of the event
- meeting times and places
- when the final numbers are due
- taste test date
- site inspection date

Contact person
- the name and phone number of the contact person for the banquet office
- the name and phone number of the caterer who will be working with you directly
- get an after hours or emergency number

Charges, fees, and deposits
- per person cost
- any discounts that apply
- whether you will pay for a specific number of guests or whether you will leave the tab open and pay for the numbers of guests actually served

Methods of payment accepted
- cash, personal or committee checks, billing on account, credit cards, money order

Payment schedule
- when deposits are due
- payments in installments
- when final payment is due
- interest (if charged)
- when deposit is returned if not applied to the final bill

Not to exceed clause
- avoid leaving any open-ended charges such as administrative fees
- even if you allow for walk-ins, have a way to keep track of how many people attended and pay only for what was actually served

Extra charges
- labor charges, gratuities
- corking, clean up, dessert table, cake cutting fees
- coffee or tea service fees

Cancellation Policy
- no penalties if you cancel before a specified date
- if you cancel after that date, payment of agreed upon expenses
- if the caterer cancels, payment of expenses incurred in finding another caterer

Deadlines or due dates
- when final numbers are due to the caterer
- time serving should begin and end
- time the tables should be cleared (in time for a presentation or entertainment)

Deliveries or pickup
- who will be in charge of delivery or pickup of any items (i.e. special cake from a baker, etc.)

Shipping method
- If food is to be shipped to you, by which method — USPS, UPS, registered, insured, overnight

Staffing or Equipment to be Used
- the name of the chef who will prepare the food
- number of serving personnel
- how personnel will be dressed

Staff's responsibilities
- if your caterer is also setting up your banquet tables or serving tables, how the tables will look and be decorated

Committee's responsibilities
- provide the caterer with the rules of the facility including starting and ending times and cooking, serving or decorating rules
- who has the authority to change menus or add additional meals to your final count

Non-Performance Penalty
- if inadequate staffing causes delays, your schedule may be affected. If late or delayed service means that your band can only play 3 hours instead of 4, for example, perhaps the caterer should pick up the cost of the 4th hour
- if there's a shortage of food, you might want to ask for a reduction in price

Catering Interview Checklist

Company Name:

Address:

Contact Name: Phone: Fax:

E-mail: URL:

Caterer's experience

Professional association memberships _____

Chef_____   Credentials_____

License_____   Insurance_____

Menus available   Per/person cost

Specialties _____

Taxes_____ Cake-Cutting_____ Coffee/Tea Service_____ Cleanup_____

Kitchen Facilities   Equipment Condition

Sit Down		Buffet	
Room Setup	Staffing needs	Room Setup	Staffing needs
Time allotted for service _____		Time allotted for service _____	
Light Menu/Snacks		**Coffee/Tea Service**	
Room Setup	Staffing needs	Room Setup	Staffing needs
Time allotted for service _____		Time allotted for service _____	

Catering Interview Checklist

Themes

Serving Tables

Food tray replacement _____

Decorations

Table skirts _____ Centerpieces _____ Seat covers _____

Serving staff

Hourly rate _____ Gratuity _____
Dress code _____ Oversight _____
Hiring requirements _____ Alcohol policy _____

Special services

Food special requests _____
Taste test of your menu _____ Time/date _____

Facility

Familiar with the facility _____
Understands facility policies _____
Available for a facility walk-through _____

Preliminary numbers due	Final numbers due

Client list/references

Billing Data

Deposit date _____ Deposit amount _____
Deposit date _____ Deposit amount _____
Final payment due _____ Final payment amount _____
Payment methods accepted _____

Food Amount Matrix Menu Planner

	Breakfast	Brunch	Lunch	Early Afternoon	Late Afternoon	6PM start	7PM start	8PM start
Hors D'oeuvres	0	0	0	4-6	6-8	10-12	8-10	4-6
Meats	2	3	4	2	4	6	6	2
Soup	0	1	2	2	1	3	1	1
Salads	0	0	3	2	2	4	3	1
Salad Dressing	0	0	3	2	2	3	3	1
Vegetables	0	2	3	3	2	4	3	2
Fruits	4	3	2	2	2	3	4	2
Cheeses	.5	.5	2	1	1	2	1	1
Breads/ Rolls	2.	1	1.5	1	1	2	1	1
Crackers	0	3	6	3	3	6	6	3
Butter	2	1.5	1.5	1	1	2	1.5	1
Dessert	.5	1	3	2	2	4	4	5

Are you planning to provide meals without the help of a caterer? This food matrix is a reflection of catering industry recommendations and should help you plan adequate amounts.

Legend

Hors d'oeuvres — pieces per person per hour

Soup — cups per person

Breads, Rolls, Crackers — pieces per person

Dessert — ounces per person

Meats, Vegetables, Salads, Fruits, Cheeses — ounces per person

Salad Dressing — tablespoons per person

Butter — pats per person

Table Settings Equipment List

Plates

- [ ] Show
- [ ] Dinner
- [ ] Salad
- [ ] Dessert
- [ ] Flat
- [ ] Rimmed

- [ ] Soup bowls
- [ ] Cups/saucers
- [ ] Consomme cups/saucers
- [ ] Demitasse cups/saucers
- [ ] Dinner knives
- [ ] Fish knives
- [ ] Dinner forks

- [ ] Fish forks
- [ ] Salad forks
- [ ] Dessert forks
- [ ] Soup spoons
- [ ] Dessert spoons
- [ ] Tea spoons
- [ ] Demitasse spoons

Pot Luck/Picnic Supplies Checklist

Assignment List
- ☐ Entrees
- ☐ Salads
- ☐ Side dishes
- ☐ Breads
- ☐ Desserts
- ☐ Appetizers

Cooking Utensils
- ☐ Tongs
- ☐ Sharp knife
- ☐ Whisk
- ☐ Meat fork
- ☐ Spatula
- ☐ Can opener

Serving/Eating Utensils
- ☐ Forks
- ☐ Knives
- ☐ Platters
- ☐ Spoons
- ☐ Bowls

Warmers
- ☐ Chafing dishes
- ☐ Sterno/canned fuel

Coolers
- ☐ Ice chests
- ☐ Ice/dry ice

Cooking
- ☐ Grill
- ☐ Matches/lighter
- ☐ Baking soda (fire safety)
- ☐ Bottle opener/corkscrew
- ☐ Charcoal/wood chips
- ☐ Charcoal starter
- ☐ Oils/seasonings
- ☐ Cutting board

Table
- ☐ Table cloths/blankets
- ☐ Plates
- ☐ Napkins/moist towelettes
- ☐ Cups/glasses

Garnishes
- ☐ Pickles
- ☐ Greens

Condiments
- ☐ Ketchup
- ☐ Onions
- ☐ Mayonnaise
- ☐ Salt/pepper
- ☐ Mustard
- ☐ Relish
- ☐ Salsa
- ☐ Sugar/sugar substitute

Clean Up
- ☐ Food wrap
- ☐ Trash bags
- ☐ Paper towels/rags
- ☐ Food storage/ziplock bags
- ☐ Removal to dump site
- ☐ Water

Chapter 18

Whetting Your Whistle:
The Drinks

 hether you're knocking back a cold one or sipping on tea, beverages are important to the festivities. There are probably as wide a variety in tastes for beverages as there are for food, so offer beverage choices including alcoholic beverages, coffee or tea, soft drinks, juices and bottled water.

At most events you can plan to serve alcoholic and non-alcoholic beverages such as soft drinks, tea and coffee. The biggest beverage decision, budgetwise, is whether or not to serve alcohol. Alcohol is more expensive than non-alcoholic drinks and the greater the variety you include in the inventory, the bigger the budget. Guests might enjoy specialty coffees, a latte, flavored syrups or liqueurs to put in the coffee. You may want to serve beverages to fit a theme. Fruity rum drinks might be just the thing for a Calypso theme.

For each event, you must decide whether you'll negotiate beverage service as a package with your facility or catering, whether you'll hire an independent beverage service, whether the committee will provide the beverages or whether guests will provide their own. Hiring a beverage service will relieve you of the liability of serving alcohol, but providing the beverages yourselves can create a significant source of funds.

In this chapter you'll find information to help you decide which beverages to serve, how you'll serve them, and whether the ticket prices will cover the cost or whether guests will pay for drinks themselves. We'll also give you tips to make working with a beverage service a breeze.

Bar Setup Checklist

Mixers

- [ ] Clamato/Tomato juice
- [ ] Cola/7-UP
- [ ] Cranberry juice
- [ ] Ginger ale
- [ ] Grapefruit/Orange juice
- [ ] Lemon/Lime juice
- [ ] Sparkling water
- [ ] Tonic water

Garnishes

- [ ] Bitters
- [ ] Black pepper
- [ ] Celery
- [ ] Cinnamon powder/sticks
- [ ] Grenadine syrup
- [ ] Jalapeno peppers
- [ ] Lemon/lime slices
- [ ] Maraschino cherries
- [ ] Margarita salt
- [ ] Mint sprigs
- [ ] Nutmeg
- [ ] Olives
- [ ] Onions
- [ ] Orange/Lemon/Lime slices
- [ ] Sugar
- [ ] Tobasco sauce
- [ ] Worcestershire sauce

Bar Equipment

- [ ] Blender
- [ ] Bottle opener
- [ ] Champagne pliers
- [ ] Citrus reamer
- [ ] Coasters
- [ ] Cocktail napkins
- [ ] Corkscrew
- [ ] Cutting board
- [ ] Funnels
- [ ] Garbage can/bags
- [ ] Garnish bowls
- [ ] Glassware
- [ ] Ice buckets
- [ ] Ice scoops/tongs
- [ ] Jiggers
- [ ] Lemon/lime squeezers
- [ ] Long-handled bar spoons
- [ ] Measuring cups/spoons
- [ ] Mixing glasses/pitchers
- [ ] Nutmeg graters
- [ ] Paper towels
- [ ] Paring knife
- [ ] Pepper mill
- [ ] Shakers
- [ ] Strainers
- [ ] Sponges
- [ ] Serving trays

Bar/Beverage Service Interview Checklist

Company Name:

Address:

Contact Name: Phone: Fax:

E-mail: URL:

Beverage Service's experience

Professional association memberships _____

Bartenders _____

Credentials _____

Liquor license _____ Liability insurance _____

Policy on serving intoxicated patrons_____

Policy on checking IDs of minors_____

Drink menus available   Per/person cost

Taxes _____ Corking fees _____ Additional equipment _____

Special requests _____Special equipment _____

Bar supplies _____

Inventory _____

Inventory reconciliation _____

Cash Bar		Open Bar	
Bar Setup	Staffing needs	Bar Setup	Staffing needs

Self-Service Bar		Coffee/Tea Service	
Room Setup	Staffing needs	Room Setup	Staffing needs

Bar/Beverage Service Checklist

Specialties

Themes

Serving area

Beverage service staff

Hourly rate _____ Gratuity _____
Dress code _____ Oversight _____
Hiring requirements _____ Alcohol policy _____

Special services

Facility

Familiar with the facility _____
Understands facility policies _____
Available for a facility walk-through _____

Preliminary numbers due	Final numbers due

Client list/references

Billing Data

Deposit date _____ Deposit amount _____
Deposit date _____ Deposit amount _____
Final payment due _____ Final payment amount _____
Payment methods accepted _____

Signing a Contract with a Beverage Service

Consider the following before you fill out an order form or negotiate a contract with a beverage service:

Precise description of service or product

- type of bar setup, and any changes in type of service, that might occur during the event
- types of liquors and non-alcoholic drinks to be served
- how much inventory will be kept in the bar including the name of well and brand name liquors
- whether there will be a tip jar on the bar or if the gratuity be included in the overall bill
- whether there is a minimum purchase over time or a minimum total volume sold

Dates, places, times

- date and location of the event(s)
- time setup should begin, time bar service will begin and end, time the bar setup must be broken down
- when final numbers are due

Contact person

- the name of the beverage service manager, a phone number and whether or not that person will be in attendance the night of the reunion in case of problems
- after hours or emergency number

Charges, fees, and deposits

- prices per drink (alcoholic and non-alcoholic)
- fees for bartenders
- whether gratuities and tax are included in the fee
- how the final bill will be tallied
- any discounts that apply

Methods of payment accepted

- whether guests will be able to use tickets distributed by the committee
- whether those tickets will count toward your minimum purchase
- cash, personal or committee check, credit card, billing on account, money order

Payment schedule

- when deposits are due
- payments in installments
- when final payment is due
- interest (if charged)
- when deposit is returned if not applied to the final bill

Not to exceed clause

- not to exceed an agreed upon inventory during an open bar

Extra charges

- corking fees
- coffee and tea service fees

Cancellation Policy

- no penalties if you cancel before a specified date
- if you cancel after the no-penalty date, payment of actual expenses incurred only
- if they cancel, payment of expenses incurred in finding another beverage service

Deadlines or due dates

- when the bar will be set up and ready for service

Deliveries or pickup

- who is responsible for pick up or delivery of bar supplies and setup to the reunion site

Shipping method

- If materials, drinks or supplies are to be shipped to you, by which method —USPS, UPS, registered, insured, overnight

Staffing or Equipment to be Used

- how many bartenders will be assigned to the event
- the qualification of the bartenders
- how they will be dressed
- whether the bar setup will include blenders, soda dispensers

Staff's irresponsibilities

- who will be responsible for refusing to serve intoxicated guests
- who will check IDs
- who will take drink tickets
- whether or not the staff will collect money or tickets

Committee's responsibilities

- to establish a policy on the service of intoxicated guests
- who has the authority to open more bottles or increase the bar inventory during the reunion
- who will supervise the initial and final count of the inventory

Non-Performance Penalty

- suggest a reduction in price should they run out of inventory or have inadequate staffing for the event

Beverage Amount Matrix

The estimates below are for the first hour's consumption. Amounts fall off significantly in each subsequent hour.

	Breakfast	Brunch	Lunch	Early Afternoon	Late Afternoon	Dinner	Cocktail Hour	Dessert
Coffee/ Tea	3	3	1	O	O	1	2	1-3
Soft Drinks	O	.5-1	2	2	2-3	1-2	1	.5-1
(kids)	O	1	2	2-3	2-3	2	1	O
Fruit Juices	2-3	2-3	O	O	O	O	1	O
(kids)	2-3	2-3	2-3	2-3	2-3	2-3	2-3	1
Beer	O	O	1-2	2-3	2-3	2-3	2-3	1-2
Mixed Drinks	1	2	.5-1	.5-1	.5-1	2-3	2-3	1-2
Wine	O	.5-1	1	.5-1	.5-1	1-2	2-3	1-2
Champagne	1	O	O	O	O	1	1	1

Are you planning to provide beverages without the help of a beverage service? This beverage matrix is a reflection of beverage industry recommendations and should help you plan for adequate amounts.

Champagne Bottle Sizing Chart

Magnum	=	2 bottles
Jeroboam	=	4 bottles
Rehoboam	=	6 bottles
Methuselah	=	8 bottles
Salmanazar	=	12 bottles
Balthazar	=	16 bottles
Nebuchadnezzar	=	20 bottles

Chapter 19

A Blast from the Past: Memorabilia

There's *nothing* better to start guests reminiscing and to set the mood for your reunion than memorabilia. Memorabilia is anything that will generate a memory; something you can touch or see, feel or hear. Think about the memories that come up when you hear the most popular song from your graduation year. What memories surface when you see the program from a play you were in? Would friends recognize you today if they saw a photograph of you in your uniform? Who do you remember when you see the insignia from your association? What do you feel when you hear the songs that were playing the day you arrived home from the service? How about when you re-read the headlines from the day your team won the national championship? Who do you remember when you see your company's logo? See how many memories came back with just a paragraph? Memorabilia is an incredible reminder of the past.

Take the time to incorporate memorabilia into your reunion. It's a sure *winner* with your guests and great fun for the committee members in charge of locating and gathering the items. Whether you use memorabilia as decorations or souvenirs, for your invitations or website — memorabilia is *the* thing that distinguishes a reunion from other gatherings.

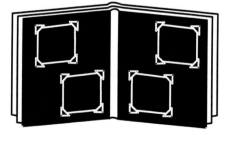Whether it represents a year in time or an era, memorabilia is everywhere. Every reunion has some type of memorabilia that will be meaningful to the people who will attend. Objects, artifacts, pictures, printed materials, music, audio messages, video or film images all make good reminders. Weave memorabilia into your reunion!

Sample Copyright Permission Letters

We are planning a reunion of _____ consisting of approximately ____ participants. We would like to include a passage from your book (see below) in our reunion's memory book. The book will be given to participants at the reunion only and have limited distribution.

Material to be reprinted: _____

Title: _____

Author: _____

Copyright date and holder: _____

Page_____ Line_____ to Page_____ Line_____

Permission Granted by: _____

Please return this form in the self-enclosed stamped envelope provided.

Thank you. _____
             (a representative of the_____ reunion committee).

We are planning a reunion of _____ consisting of approximately ____ participants. We would like to play a song from your album (see below) at our reunion.

Song: _____

Album Title: _____

Artist: _____

Copyright date and holder: _____

Permission Granted by: _____

Please return this form in the self-enclosed stamped envelope provided.

Thank you. _____
             (a representative of the_____ reunion committee).

We need the following memorabilia for the reunion
Tell us what you can contribute

Audio	Photographs

Magazines or Newspapers	Film or video

Souvenirs	Stuff

Name	
Address	
City	State	Zip
Phone	E-mail:

Creating a Memorable Audio History

Phrases to keep the conversation going ...

Tell me more about ...

Explain ...

Go on ...

What happened next? ...

What did you do ...

How did you ...

Your Early Years ...

When were you born?

Where were you born?

What's your given name?

Were you named after someone?

Do you have any nicknames?

What was your favorite toy?

What kind of games did you play?

Your Family ...

What kind of things did your family do together?

What relative did you spend the most time with as a child?

How did your family spend weekends?

What after school activities did you and your siblings participate in?

What was the most common topic of conversation at home?

Your House ...

Where did you live as a child?

Who lived there with you?

Did you ever move?

How old were you when you moved?

What was it like going to a new school?

Describe your favorite house

Describe your room

How was it decorated?

What was your favorite room in the house?

Friends ...

Who were your childhood friends?

Who was your best friend?

What was your favorite activity with friends?

Where are your childhood friends now?

Pets ...

Did you have any pets?

What kind of animals were they?

What were their names?

Who named them?

What did you do with your pets?

Did you have a favorite pet?

Community/World Events

Who was President when you were a kid?

What important events took place when you were a kid?

What was the craziest fad when you were a kid?

What were the fashions when you were a kid?

What do you still have today that you wore back then?

What kind of music did you listen to?

What kind of dances did you do?

What was on television/radio when you were a kid?

What did people do for entertainment?

What sports were popular?

What teams won championships?

Kid Favorites ...

What was your favorite food or drink?

What was your favorite color?

Who was your childhood hero?

What was your favorite song?

What was your favorite movie?

What was your favorite time of the year?

What was your favorite TV show?

What was your favorite book?

Chapter 20

In Memory ... :
Remembering Those Who Have Gone Before

When we speak to reunion committees about doing a memorial or a tribute, we often hear: "Why would we want to do that? A reunion is supposed to be a party!" A tribute to deceased members doesn't have to be maudlin or morbid so don't be afraid that a memorial display of some kind will create discomfort for guests or put a damper on the party. A tribute can be as simple as a framed photograph or a moment of silence.

Almost every reunion group will be faced with the loss of some members. Some groups have lost many. Remembering, as a part of the reunion, can be life affirming — a source of comfort for the living. Memories shared are tremendously healing. Include the family members of the deceased in your plans. Ask them to participate in any tribute or memorials you're planning or to join the reunion celebration. Your tribute can be something simple like a moment of silence or something more elaborate like a memorial service. A tribute to your deceased members won't put a damper on the party.

There aren't many customs or protocols for tributes or memorials during reunions. The military has burial traditions and families sometimes plan activities around Memorial Day, but most reunion groups will have to establish traditions of their own.

In this chapter you'll find information to help you choose a memorial, show you how to involve the deceased member's family, help you choose a vendor for a lasting memorial and give you some suggestions for dealing with reactions to the news of a death.

Become a sponsored vendor!

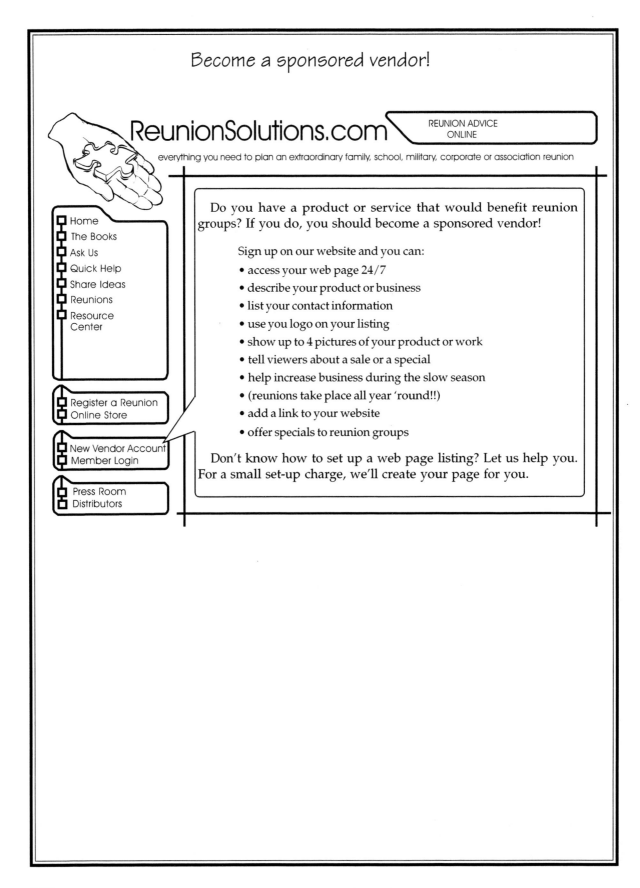

ReunionSolutions.com
REUNION ADVICE
ONLINE

everything you need to plan an extraordinary family, school, military, corporate or association reunion

- Home
- The Books
- Ask Us
- Quick Help
- Share Ideas
- Reunions
- Resource Center

- Register a Reunion
- Online Store

- New Vendor Account
- Member Login

- Press Room
- Distributors

Do you have a product or service that would benefit reunion groups? If you do, you should become a sponsored vendor!

Sign up on our website and you can:
- access your web page 24/7
- describe your product or business
- list your contact information
- use you logo on your listing
- show up to 4 pictures of your product or work
- tell viewers about a sale or a special
- help increase business during the slow season
- (reunions take place all year 'round!!)
- add a link to your website
- offer specials to reunion groups

Don't know how to set up a web page listing? Let us help you. For a small set-up charge, we'll create your page for you.

Script for Contacting Family Members of the Deceased

Explain why you're writing. Tell the family who you are and that you're planning a reunion
- We, the _____ reunion committee are planning an upcoming reunion.
- The _____ year reunion for _____ is coming up on _____

Explain that you're planning a memorial
- In loving memory of_____ we're planning_____
- We're planning _____ to honor_____
- The memorial will be held _____
- The memorial display will be shown _____
- List the memorial activities you're planning
- The _____ will be placed at _____ on _____ as a permanent remembrance.
- The plaque will read _____

Request the help you want
- We're putting together _____ and here's how you can help.
- If you would like to contribute _____
- We have enclosed _____
- Feel free to share our request with other family members.

Invite the family to the reunion
- We'd like to extend an invitation to the reunion to you.
- We'd like you to be our honorary guests.
- We're sure many of _____'s (classmates, colleagues, shipmates) would like to see you to share their remembrances of_____ with you.
- You played an important role not only in _____'s life but in ours as well.

Closing
- We're sensitive to your loss, and realize our request may bring back difficult memories for you.
- We remember_____ fondly and wanted you to know of our memorial plans.
- We would appreciate any_____ you would like to contribute.
- We wanted you to know that_____ is not forgotten.

Suggestions for a Tribute

A tribute is a laudatory speech praising someone who has died.

Gather your ideas about what to say

- Collect facts about the person such as their age, spouse's name, marriage date, placed they lived, names of children, siblings or parents, profession, etc.
- Express your love and remembrance of the deceased.
- Show how the deceased had an effect on your life.
- Think about the stories you remember.
- What made the deceased laugh or cry?
- Think about sayings or typical behavior that captures the spirit of the deceased.
- Talk with other people who remember the deceased and include their comments as well.

Think about a theme for the tribute

- A theme helps listeners to see patterns and what was familiar in the deceased's life.
- Think about traits that were consistent throughout the deceased's life.
- Think about a metaphor or an analogy you can use to describe the contributions of the deceased.

Organize the material

- Write your notes in bullet form. That way, you won't be tempted to read them like a script. Reading this way sounds unnatural and won't allow you to interact with the audience.
- Talk to the audience as if they were sitting with you at your kitchen table.
- Speak in plain, simple language.

Practice your delivery

- If you're not used to speaking in public, practice until you feel comfortable.
- Read the tribute into a tape recorder and play it back.
- Read the tribute in front of a video camera and watch the tape.
- Keep practicing until you're comfortable with the words and until your movements are natural.

Ask for backup

- If you feel that you might break down during the tribute, ask another person to act as your backup. Knowing you have someone waiting in the wings to help may be all you need to stay calm.

Memorials Vendor Interview Checklist

Company Name:

Address:

Contact Name: Phone: Fax:

E-mail: URL:

Product line

Suggested wording

Delivery/placement services

Returns policy

Client list/references

Billing Data

Deposit date _____   Deposit amount_____

Deposit date _____   Deposit amount_____

Final payment due _____   Final payment amount_____

Payment methods accepted _____

Signing a Contract with a Memorials Vendor

Consider the following before you fill out an order form with a memorials manufacturer:

Precise description of service or product

- make certain that they are using the same materials to produce your items as they showed you in the sample
- product number
- catalog page or issue
- whether proofs or examples will be provided
- an assurance of quality to the committee's satisfaction
- shipping and packaging to prevent damage
- specifications sheet from the manufacturer

Dates, places, times

- date of the reunion
- when the order will be placed
- date of delivery
- turnaround time

Contact person

- contact name and phone number of the person who took the order

Charges, fees and deposits

- per item costs
- any discounts for quantity
- any interest charges

Methods of payment accepted

- cash, personal or committee check, credit card, billing on account, money order

Payment schedule

- when deposits are due
- when the final payment is due
- whether you can pay in installments
- when deposits will be returned if they are not to be applied to the final bill

Not to exceed clause

- if they plan to produce an overage to cover any products with defects, include a not-to-exceed clause to ensure that you're not paying for extras that you don't want

Extra charges

- fees for direct shipment to the place where the memorial will be permanently located
- permanent installment fees
- design fees
- setup fees
- shipping and handling

Cancellation Policy

- date before which either party can cancel without penalty
- policy for credits and returns
- penalty if they cancel after the designated date
- penalty if you cancel after the designated date

Deadlines or due dates

- date for seeing proofs
- delivery date
- permanent placement date

Deliveries or pickup

- whether the committee will be responsible for picking up the memorial or whether it will be delivered
- whether the memorial will be shipped directly to the area where it will be place permanently

Shipping method

- USPS, UPS, overnight, insured, registered
- how the memorial will be packaged to avoid damage
- if damage or loss does occur during shipping, how items will be replaced and how quickly they will be delivered

Staffing or Equipment to be Used

- specify the manufacturing process to be used

Staff's responsibilities

- whether or not they have a backup supplier in case the manufacturer can't deliver in time for the reunion

Committee's responsibilities

- whether the committee will need to provide the wording or design prior to production
- who has the authority to make changes to the order

Non-Performance Penalty

- payment of express charges if the manufacturing is delayed
- if they cancel after the agreed upon non-penalty date, they should pay for any charges that incur in finding another memorials manufacturer
- if you cancel after the non-penalty date, you should pay only for costs actually incurred
- if merchandise is unsatisfactory or the wrong item is shipped, you may consider withholding payment until the new item is delivered and inspected

Chapter 21

Somebody Ought to Say Something ...: Presentations and Entertainment

Presentations and entertainment go hand in hand with reunions. At your initial gathering, plan for a welcome and announcements. Your guests will want to hear from the committee to kick off the reunion. Your other events may call for something different — entertainment, a speaker, awards or a multimedia show. You may find that you'll be planning a presentation of some type for each reunion event.

A basic presentation plan incorporates what the presentation will consist of, at what point during the event the presentation will begin, the environment in which the presentation will take place and how long the presentation will last.

Once you've carved out a block of time in your schedule for entertainment or presentations, it's time to figure out what you'll include. Different events call for different presentation styles, so you may end up using many presentations during your reunion.

In this chapter you'll find information to help you carve out time during your reunion activities for a presentation, show you what kinds of presentations are possible, illustrate how to use an emcee to pull together different presentation elements and give you tips for hiring a speaker or entertainer should you need one.

'Award' Winning Ideas

Personal awards

Changed the least
Changed the most
Most recently married
Longest married
Most (number of times) married
Married sweethearts (classmates or members married to each other)
Most eligible ...
Most recent parents
Most children
Multiple births (twins, triplets)
First grandparent
Most grandchildren
Most unusual occupation
First to retire
Highest rank
Most number of years (with a company or in the service)
Longest distance traveled to the reunion
Longest distance traveled to an exotic place
Most (number of times) moved

Reunion Awards

First registration
Worst procrastinator (last registration)
Most members found
Best reunion idea
The whopper award (most creative life story)
Lobster award (best sunburn)
Most money raised
Most tickets sold

Tribute Starters

Thank you for being examples of love and care
Thank you for being an example of hard work and principled living
Thank you for always being there
Thank you for making our house a home
Thank you for wholeheartedly for being a good friend even though you had a hard time expressing it
Thank you for always rushing out the door to greet us when we arrived for a visit
Thank you for your special call of encouragement
Thank you for your patience during the difficult times
Thank you for being proud
Thank you for being one of the kindest people I've known
Thank you for being a tremendous example
Thank you for your outlook on life
Thank you for your outlook on other people
Thank you for being a leader
Thank you for being a tireless advocate
Thank you for remembering others
Thank you for representing the best in all of us

Leadership awards

Spark plug award (person who sparked the idea for the reunion)
Berry Award (for a 'Berry' good job)
Shaquille award (heads above the rest)
Measure up award (you set the standard)
Nuts award (nuts about the job)
Order of the bear (you bear up under pressure)
Live saver award (you saved us)
Hat's off award (we take our hats off to you)
Right Foot award (you got us off on the right foot)
A note to start on (for those who got us going)
Egg award (for an 'egg'cellent job)
Airplane award (you really helped us fly)
Tea bag award (you were 'tea'-riffic)
Band Aid (you really helped fix us up)
Globe award (for the world's best)
Maze award (you're a-maze-ing)
Hat award (hat's off to ...)
Magic award (you worked magic)
Lion award (it was a roaring success)
Shovel award (for digging in to help)
Tape award (you really stuck to it)
Planet award (out of this world)
Chalkboard award (chalk up a great reunion)
Steak award (well done)
Carabiner award (hang in there)
Fire engine award (you came to our rescue)
Frog award (you really hopped to it)
Marker award (you were re-'mark'-able)
Maze award (you were a-'maze'-ing)
Neon award (de-'light'-ful)
Baby Doe award (you were 'matchless')
Egg beater award (you were unbeatable)
Plunger award (for plunging right in)
Pencil award (write on!)
Seal award (our seal of approval)
Lightbulb award (bright idea)
Recipe award (all the right ingredients)
Rope award (for tying up loose ends)
Crossword award (no words to describe you)
Tree award ('tree'-mendous)
Royal Flush award (you're a great hand)
Reflector award (you reflect our spirit)
Notepad award (most noteworthy)
Compass award (you lead the way)
Horn award (music to our ears)
Bear award (you gave your 'beary' best)
Glider award (smooth sailing)
Newspaper award (good news)
Bundle award (thanks a bundle)
Cheese grater award ('grate' job)
Golf tee award ('Tee'-riffic job)
Compass award (you lead the way)
Broom award (you swept us away)
Scissors award (you're cut out for the job)
Sandpaper award (you smoothed the way)
Needle-Thread award (you kept us in stitches)
Pear award (for a really great 'pear')
Kite award (you had us flying high)
Key award (you were the key to our success)
Bean award (you've 'been' great)
Pig award (for the biggest ham)

**Consider awarding a winner and a runner up

Presentation Plan

Time	Program Element

Presenter Tip Sheet

Public Speaking Basics

- [ ] Prepare, Prepare, Prepare
- [ ] Check your visual image
- [ ] Take the stage with authority
- [ ] Maintain eye contact
- [ ] Watch your body language
- [ ] Empty your pockets
- [ ] Vary your pace, pitch and volume
- [ ] Speak with confidence
- [ ] Use notes unobtrusively
- [ ] Don't read what's on the screen
- [ ] Plan your exit
- [ ] End memorably

AV Equipment Checklist

- [ ] Amplifier
- [ ] Freight elevator
- [ ] Lectern
- [ ] Microphones
- [ ] Satellite transmission
- [ ] Slide/Film/Video/Computer Projector
- [ ] Staff for operation
- [ ] Staging
- [ ] Audio mixer
- [ ] Front/Rear Projection
- [ ] Lighting
- [ ] Phone line
- [ ] Screen
- [ ] Sound System
- [ ] Staff for setup
- [ ] VCR/DVD Player

Presenter Supplies List

- [ ] Presentation
- [ ] Hard copy of the presentation
- [ ] Equipment backup
- [ ] Duct tape
- [ ] Flipcharts/Paper
- [ ] Masking tape
- [ ] Pointer/lighted pointer
- [ ] Whiteboards
- [ ] Extra copy of the presentation
- [ ] Extra copy in a different format
- [ ] Chalk
- [ ] Easel
- [ ] Handouts
- [ ] Pens/Pencils
- [ ] Write-on-Wipe-off pens

Technical Rehearsal Checklist

- [ ] Access to staging
- [ ] AV Screen height
- [ ] Cords taped down
- [ ] Lighting dimmed
- [ ] Stage lighting
- [ ] Audio check for dead spots
- [ ] Clear field of vision
- [ ] Equipment working
- [ ] Spotlights off
- [ ] Stairs lighting

Presenter Personal Supplies List

- [ ] Breath mints
- [ ] Wrinkle remover spray
- [ ] Lint brush
- [ ] Static guard

Speaker Interview Checklist

Company Name:

Address:

Contact Name: Phone: Fax:

E-mail: URL:

Speaker's experience

Professional association memberships _____

Speaker's portfolio/demonstration materials

Message: _____ Delivery _____ Authenticity _____

Typical program length

Speaker/entertainer's fees

Hourly _____ Total _____ Travel _____ Supplies _____ Per-diem _____

Equipment needed

Special requirements

Dressing room_____ Back of the room sales _____

Copyrights

Video/audio taping_____ Permission to reproduce handouts _____

Backup plans

Client list/references

Billing Data

    Deposit date _____ Deposit amount_____

    Deposit date _____ Deposit amount_____

    Final payment due _____ Final payment amount_____

    Payment methods accepted _____

Signing a Contract with a Speaker

Consider the following before you fill out an order form or negotiate a contract with a speaker:

Precise description of service or product

- topic of discussion
- approximate length of talk
- whether speaker will make own travel arrangements
- whether copyrights will be assigned to the reunion for video, CD-ROM or reunion website use
- whether speaker will be accompanied by family or guests
- arrival time and flight number, departure time, airline
- whether you'll need to have someone meet the speaker at the airport
- special accommodations required (secretarial, babysitting, security)
- backup plans

Dates, places, times

- date of the reunion
- location of the reunion
- start and end times of the event
- arrival time at the reunion
- time speech will begin and the length it will run

Contact person

- speaker's name and number
- contact person's name and number (in the event that the speaker uses a publicist or booking agent)
- get an after hours or emergency number

Charges, fees, and deposits

- speaking fee or hourly rate
- deposits
- which expenses will be reimbursed
- any discounts that apply

Methods of payment accepted

- cash, personal or committee check, credit card, billing on account, money order

Payment schedule

- when deposits are due
- whether payments may be made in installments and when final payment is due
- when deposit is returned if not applied to the final bill

Not to exceed clause

- you may want to put a limit on expenses if you are paying travel and meals for your speaker

Extra charges

- AV equipment
- travel expenses
- per diem meal expenses
- security expenses

Cancellation Policy

- if you cancel, payment of actual expenses incurred only
- no penalties if you cancel before a specified date
- if they cancel, payment of expenses incurred in finding another speaker

Deadlines or due dates

- when biography information for the speaker's introduction will be given to the committee
- when the speaker will arrive and how long the speaker will speak

Deliveries or pickup

- who is responsible for delivery or pickup of the speaker's materials or AV equipment

Shipping method

- If any materials or AV Equipment are to be shipped to you, by which method — USPS, UPS, registered, insured, overnight

Staffing or Equipment to be Used

- whether the speaker requires specific AV equipment, lighting or sound system

Staff's responsibilities

- what materials will be provided by the speaker
- biographical information to use for their introduction

Committee's responsibilities

- all arrangements and instructions in writing
- whether committee will make speaker's travel arrangements
- whether someone will meet the speaker at the airport
- what equipment will be provided by the committee
- who has the authority to make changes to the agreement with the speaker

Non-Performance Penalty

- replacement cost if the speaker cancels at the last minute

Entertainer Interview Checklist

Company Name:

Address:

Contact Name: Phone: Fax:

E-mail: URL:

Entertainer's experience

Professional association memberships _____

Entertainer's portfolio/demonstration materials

Typical Program Length

Speaker/Entertainer's Fees

Hourly _____ Total _____ Travel _____ Supplies ____ Per-diem _____

Equipment Needed

Special requirements

Dressing room_____ Back of the room sales _____

Copyrights

Video/audio taping _____

Backup plans

Client list/references

Billing Data

Deposit date _____ Deposit amount_____

Deposit date _____ Deposit amount_____

Final payment due _____ Final payment amount_____

Payment methods accepted _____

Signing a Contract with an Entertainer

Consider the following before you fill out an order form or negotiate a contract with an entertainer:

Precise description of service or product

- approximate length of performance and breaks
- special accommodations required (secretarial, babysitting, security)
- whether copyrights will be assigned to the reunion for video, CD-ROM or reunion website use

Dates, places, times

- date and location of the reunion
- start and end times of the event
- arrival time for setup
- time performance will begin

Contact person

- entertainer's name and phone number
- contact person's name and number (in the event that the entertainer uses a booking agent)
- after hours or emergency number

Charges, fees, and deposits

- performance fee
- deposits
- which expenses will be reimbursed
- extended performance fee
- any discounts that apply

Methods of payment accepted

- cash, personal or committee check, credit card, billing on account, money order

Payment schedule

- when deposits are due
- whether payments may be made in installments and when final payment is due
- when deposit is returned if not applied to the final bill

Not to exceed clause

- you may want to put a limit on expenses if you are paying travel and meals

Extra charges

- equipment
- travel
- per diem for meals
- security

Cancellation Policy

- if you cancel, payment of actual expenses incurred only
- no penalties if you cancel before a specified date
- if they cancel, payment of expenses incurred in finding another entertainer

Deadlines or due dates

- when biography information for the speaker's introduction will be given to the committee
- when the speaker will arrive and how long the speaker will speak

Deliveries or pickup

- who is responsible for delivery or pickup of the speaker's materials or AV equipment

Shipping method

- If any materials or AV Equipment are to be shipped to you, by which method — USPS, UPS, registered, insured, overnight

Staffing or Equipment to be Used

- whether the entertainer requires specific equipment as well as outlets, power draw, microphones or lighting needed

Staff's responsibilities

- what materials will be provided by the entertainer
- biographical information to use for an introduction

Committee's responsibilities

- all arrangements and instructions in writing
- whether committee will make entertainer's travel arrangements
- whether someone will meet the entertainer at the airport
- what equipment will be provided by the committee
- who has the authority to make changes to the agreement with the entertainer

Non-Performance Penalty

- replacement cost if the entertainer cancels at the last minute

Multimedia Storyboard

Presentation _____

Description _____

Clip Number _____

Video 1	
Video 2	
Audio 1	
Audio 2	
Titles	
Transitions	

Clip Number _____

Video 1	
Video 2	
Audio 1	
Audio 2	
Titles	
Transitions	

Multimedia Storyboard

Presentation _____

Description _____

Clip Number _____

Video 1

Video 2

Audio 1

Audio 2

Titles

Transitions

Clip Number _____

Video 1

Video 2

Audio 1

Audio 2

Titles

Transitions

Chapter 22

There's a Song in the Air: Music

Music is a way to take you back in time — to set the scene for an era. It's a part of your memorabilia, your nostalgia. Play music whenever it will enhance what's already happening at the reunion — to complement the entertainment, for dancing, to create an ambiance or to get guests thinking about events that were taking place 'way back when.'

Before you make any decisions about music, though, keep in mind that reunions are *primarily* about reconnecting. There will be times when your guests will be more interested in catching up with old friends, colleagues or family than in listening to music. We hear it again and again — the single most common complaint about reunions is music that's too loud to talk. Again, reunions are about reconnecting. It's hard to do that if you can't hold a conversation.

So what type of music should you have at a reunion? There are as many different tastes for music as there are for food. Even though music is a very powerful reminder of the past, plan for music to fit the event as a whole. You might be planning an event where the music will take center stage — for after-dinner dancing or a "Name that Tune" contest. Or maybe you want music to stir memories, to fit a theme or to play in the background just to create an ambiance.

In this chapter you'll find information to help you choose music, coordinate with your facility, develop a playlist, record music or hire a band or a disc jockey.

Music Copyrights' Checklist

Contact the music licensing organizations below to inquire about music licenses

American Association of Composers, Authors and Publishers
One Lincoln Plaza
New York, NY 10023
www.ascap.com
E-mail: info@ascap.com
1-800-95-ASCAP

BMI-New York
320 West 57th Street
New York, NY 10019-3790
www.bmi.com
E-mail: newyork@bmi.com
(212) 586-2000

SESAC
55 Music Square East
Nashville, TN 37203
www.sesac.com
E-mail: license@sesac.com
1-800-826-9996

Sample Copyright Permission Letter

We are planning a reunion of _____ consisting of approximately ____
participants. We would like to play a song from your album (see below) at our reunion.

Song: _____

Album Title: _____

Artist: _____

Copyright date and holder: _____

Permission Granted by: _____

Please return this form in the self-enclosed stamped envelope provided.

Thank you. _____

(a representative of the _____ reunion committee).

Musicians Interview Checklist

Company Name:		
Address:		
Contact Name:	Phone:	Fax:
E-mail:	URL:	

Musicians' experience

Professional association memberships _____

Typical performance

Take requests _____

Demonstration materials

Tape _____ Video _____ Multimedia _____

Fees

Hourly _____ Travel _____ Per-diem _____

Equipment/Equipment requirements

Attire

Copyrights

Backup plans

Client list/References

Billing Data

Deposit date _____ Deposit amount _____

Deposit date _____ Deposit amount _____

Final payment due _____ Final payment amount _____

Payment methods accepted _____

Signing a Contract with Musicians

Consider the following before you negotiate a contract with a band or their agent:

Precise description of service or product

- how many members in the band
- how long breaks will be and how many breaks will be taken
- whether they will provide pre-recorded music for breaks
- what equipment they will provide (sound system) and what equipment and power requirements they have
- whether they will take requests
- whether they will decline requests at your direction
- copyright agreement
- what, if any, union requirements they have
- contingency plans

Dates, places, times

- date of the reunion
- the place of performance
- when the music should begin and end
- when the facility is available for setup or practices

Contact person

- the contact person and phone number for the band or agent
- an after-hours or emergency number

Charges, fees, and deposits

- hourly rate
- any discounts that apply

Methods of payment accepted

- cash, personal or committee check, credit card, billing on account, money order

Payment schedule

- when deposits are due
- if payments in can be made in installments
- when final payment is due
- interest (if charged)
- when deposit is returned if not applied to the final bill

Extra charges

- any extra charges for playing overtime
- travel or per diem expenses

Cancellation Policy

- no penalties if you cancel before a specified date
- if you cancel, payment of actual expenses incurred only
- if they cancel, payment of expenses incurred in finding another band

Deadlines or due dates

- by what time all setup and breakdown will be completed

Deliveries or pickup

- who is responsible for delivery or pickup of any equipment needed for the band

Shipping method

- If any equipment is to be shipped to you, by which method — USPS, UPS, registered, insured, overnight

Staffing or Equipment to be Used

- describe amplification and power requirements
- how many members are in the band

Staff's responsibilities

- what setup and equipment is needed
- what props will be provided by the band

Committee's responsibilities

- what equipment or props will be provided by the committee

Non-Performance Penalty

- suggest a reduction in final payment should a substitution of band members affect performance
- suggest a decrease in payment if the band begins late or ends early

Disc Jockey Interview Checklist

Company Name:	
Address:	
Contact Name:	Phone: Fax:
E-mail:	URL:

DJ' experience

Professional association memberships

Music specialty/typical performance

Demonstration materials

Tape _____ Video _____ Multimedia_____

Fees

Hourly _____ Travel_____ Per-diem _____

Equipment/equipment requirements

Attire

Copyrights

Backup plans

Client list/references

Billing Data

Deposit date _____ Deposit amount_____

Deposit date _____ Deposit amount_____

Final payment due _____ Final payment amount_____

Payment methods accepted _____

Signing a Contract with a Disc Jockey

Consider the following before you negotiate a contract with a DJ or their agent:

Precise description of service or product

- play list
- how long breaks will be and how many will be taken
- whether they will provide pre-recorded music for breaks
- what equipment they will provide and whether you will be able to use their equipment to make announcements
- copyright agreement
- what, if any, union requirements they have
- contingency plans

Dates, places, times

- date of the reunion
- location of the reunion
- start and end times of the event
- when the music should begin and end
- what time setup and breakdown must be complete

Contact person

- contact person and phone number of the company
- name and phone number of the DJ
- get an after hours or emergency number

Charges, fees, and deposits

- hourly rate
- any discounts that apply

Methods of payment accepted

- cash, personal or committee check, credit card, billing on account, money order

Payment schedule

- when deposits are due
- payments in installments
- when final payment is due
- interest (if charged)
- when deposit is returned if not applied to the final bill

Extra charges

- any extra charges for playing overtime
- travel or per diem expenses

Cancellation Policy

- if you cancel, payment of actual expenses incurred only
- no penalties if you cancel before a specified date
- if they cancel, payment of expenses incurred in finding another disc jockey

Deadlines or due dates

- by what time all setup and breakdown will be completed

Deliveries or pickup

- who is responsible for delivery or pickup of any equipment needed for the DJ

Shipping method

- If any equipment is to be shipped to you, by which method -- USPS, UPS, registered, insured, overnight

Staffing or Equipment to be Used

- describe amplification and power requirements

Staff's irresponsibilities

- what equipment, props will be provided by the DJ
- how the DJ will be dressed
- what announcements will be done by the DJ

Committee's responsibilities

- what equipment will be provided by the committee
- who has the authority to extend the time the DJ plays

Non-Performance Penalty

- a reduction in final payment should a substitution of music or DJ affect performance

Chapter 23

Beyond Balloons: Decorations

eunion decorating should be something more than a few balloons, streamers and centerpieces. Consider the whole space — the ceiling, the walls, the tabletops, the floors and any empty areas. The problem with many decorating schemes is that they only appeal to the visual sense — the things you can see. We'll show you how to use decorations to create an atmosphere and transform an otherwise generic space into something spectacular.

Decorations are the vehicle you'll use to create an ambiance — an atmosphere. Try to include each of the five senses — sight, sound, touch, taste and smell. Use decorations to add color, subdue or enhance existing lighting or make a room look bigger or smaller. Use your decorations to create a consistent, unifying look.

When most people think of table decorations they think of centerpieces — objects to occupy that big, empty spot in the middle of the table. Table decorations are money well spent if guests will be spending time seated at tables.

Look at the walls of your facility as a blank canvas. Maybe the wallpaper doesn't fit your theme. Maybe the paint is a drab off-white. No matter. Let the walls help transform the space.

If there are empty spaces in the room, fill them using free-standing decorations such as artifacts, exhibits, plants, screens or dividers.

In this chapter you'll find information to help you develop an indoor or an out-of-doors decorating plan, use available surfaces, incorporate your memorabilia and work with your facility to achieve decorating success.

Sponsor a reunion-planning workshop!

 ReunionSolutions.com

REUNION ADVICE
ONLINE

everything you need to plan an extraordinary family, school, military, corporate or association reunion

- Home
- The Books
- Ask Us
- Quick Help
- Share Ideas
- Reunions
- Resource Center

- Register a Reunion
- Online Store

- New Vendor Account
- Member Login

- Press Room
- Distributors

Would you, and other reunion-planning committees in your area, like some helpful one-on-one advice from the experts?

Sponsor a Reunion Solutions Workshop!

Contact other groups in your area, gather a crowd and we'll come in for a 4-hour, intensive, reunion-planning workshop where we will help you brainstorm ideas for your reunion.

How can you set up a workshop?

Send us an e-mail at:

Reunion-Doctor@ReunionSolutions.com to let us know that you're interested.

We'll send you a Workshop Setup Kit with our schedule and information to help you.

Decorations Idea Sheet

Wall decorations

Table decorations

Ceiling/floor decorations

Free-standing decorations

Setup/Cleanup Supplies List

Setup

- [ ] Tape
- [ ] Pens/Pencils
- [ ] Paintbrushes
- [ ] Glue
- [ ] Stapler
- [ ] Crepe paper
- [ ] Tablecloths
- [ ] Candles
- [ ] Confetti
- [ ] Signs
- [ ] Ribbon

- [ ] String
- [ ] Erasers
- [ ] Fabric markers
- [ ] Sponges
- [ ] Paper clips
- [ ] Tissue paper
- [ ] Table cover clips
- [ ] Banners
- [ ] Bows
- [ ] Dangling cutouts
- [ ] Disposable cameras

- [ ] Scissors
- [ ] Sharpeners
- [ ] Paper/plastic bags
- [ ] Craft knife
- [ ] Balloons
- [ ] Backdrops
- [ ] Napkins/Napkin rings
- [ ] Border trim
- [ ] Bubbles
- [ ] Garlands
- [ ] Lighting

Cleanup

- [ ] Do not throw away list
- [ ] Trashbags/ties
- [ ] Scissors
- [ ] Stain remover
- [ ] Food containers

- [ ] Transport to next event list
- [ ] Cleaning supplies
- [ ] Tape remover
- [ ] Paper towels
- [ ] Labels

- [ ] Haul away plans
- [ ] Glue remover
- [ ] Sponges
- [ ] Boxes

Balloon Retrieval Tools

- [ ] Water bottle
- [ ] Balloon weights

- [ ] Cherry picker
- [ ] Rake

- [ ] Long string/ribbon

Confetti Removal Tools

- [ ] Static remover
- [ ] Lint brushes
- [ ] Throw-away floor sweeper

Decoration Service Interview Checklist

Company Name:

Address:

Contact Name: Phone: Fax:

E-mail: URL:

Decoration service experience

Professional association memberships

Decoration service portfolio

Fabrics/custom drapery _____   Florals _____

Holiday decorations _____   Memorabilia _____

Lighting _____   Signage _____

Souvenirs _____   Stage sets _____

Fees

Design _____   Assembly _____   Labor _____

Additional services

Copyrights

Client list/references

Billing Data

Deposit date _____   Deposit amount _____

Deposit date _____   Deposit amount _____

Final payment due _____   Final payment amount _____

Payment methods accepted _____

Signing a Contract with a Decoration Service

Consider the following before you fill out an order form or negotiate a contract with a decoration service:

Precise description of service or product

- theme or design idea
- all elements that will appear at the event
- what materials will be used to construct decorations
- whether copyrights will be assigned to the reunion for video, CD-ROM or reunion website use
- staff to help set up and clean up decorations
- backup plans

Dates, places, times

- date of the reunion
- location of each reunion event
- start and end times of each event
- arrival time for setup
- vacate time

Contact person

- decorator's name and number
- contact person's name and number at the decoration service
- after hours or emergency number

Charges, fees, and deposits

- fees for design, assembly and labor
- deposits
- which expenses will be reimbursed
- any discounts that apply

Methods of payment accepted

- cash, personal or committee check, credit card, billing on account, money order

Payment schedule

- when deposits are due
- whether payments may be made in installments and when final payment is due
- when deposit is returned if not applied to the final bill

Not to exceed clause

- you may want to put a limit on expenses for materials

Extra charges

- AV equipment
- travel/transportation expenses
- staff at the facility to move equipment

Cancellation Policy

- if you cancel, payment of actual expenses incurred only
- no penalties if you cancel before a specified date
- if they cancel, payment of expenses incurred in finding another decoration service plus materials

Deadlines or due dates

- when design sketches will be given to the committee
- when the crew will arrive to setup and return for cleanup

Deliveries or pickup

- who is responsible for delivery or pickup of materials or AV equipment

Shipping method

- If any materials are to be shipped to you, by which method — USPS, UPS, registered, insured, overnight

Staffing or Equipment to be Used

- how many staff will be available for setup and cleanup and any equipment they require

Staff's responsibilities

- what materials and equipment will be provided by the decoration service

Committee's responsibilities

- all arrangements and instructions in writing
- whether members of the committee or volunteers will help with setup or cleanup
- what equipment will be provided by the committee
- who has the authority to make changes to the agreement with the decoration service

Non-Performance Penalty

- replacement cost of materials if the decoration service cancels at the last minute

Chapter 24

Collector's Edition: Souvenirs

*S*ouvenirs are lasting mementos. They help us remember. They represent affinity, belonging and identity. They're symbols or heirlooms or keepsakes and they increase the value of the reunion.

Souvenirs can be something practical to use during the reunion, be used to raise funds, create group spirit or camaraderie, bring a part of the reunion to members who can't attend or provide a remembrance for generations to come. Even if you have the ideal room, a delicious menu, the best decorations and the perfect music — without souvenirs, the reunion is missing something.

There are some souvenirs you might want to send before the reunion. Maybe a videotape of the area you'll all be traveling to will convince members to attend. Maybe a decal could accompany the invitation. Some souvenirs might sell better if buyers have a chance to look the item over before they purchase. These souvenirs should be made available for sale *during* the reunion. Other souvenirs would be better suited for use after the reunion. Any items that are breakable or bulky are good candidates to be sent after the reunion, although you'll incur mailing expenses.

Sometimes the perfect souvenir is obvious. Give away luggage tags for a travel theme, leis for a luau or beer steins for Oktoberfest. These souvenirs are the kind of *giveaway* items that are fun to receive. They can also help tie your theme together or act as a finishing touch for your decorating.

In this chapter you'll find information to help you choose souvenirs, create the least-risky financial scenario for your budget, market the souvenirs and work with souvenir manufacturers to get the products you want.

Souvenir Ideas Checklist

Event Description_____
Souvenir Ideas

Event Description_____
Souvenir Ideas

Event Description_____
Souvenir Ideas

Event Description_____
Souvenir Ideas

Event Description_____
Souvenir Ideas

Event Description_____
Souvenir Ideas

Event Description_____
Souvenir Ideas

Event Description_____
Souvenir Ideas

Souvenir Vendor Interview Checklist

Company Name:

Address:

Contact Name: Phone: Fax:

E-mail: URL:

Souvenir vendor experience

Manufacturer_____   Re-seller_____

Product line/catalog

Proofs_____   Personalized_____

Souvenir prices

Setup charges_____

Discounts_____   Premiums_____

Extra services

Drop shipping_____

Returns/damage policy

Client list/references

Billing Data

   Deposit date _____   Deposit amount_____

   Deposit date _____   Deposit amount_____

   Final payment due _____   Final payment amount_____

   Payment methods accepted _____

Signing a Contract with a Souvenir Vendor

Consider the following before you fill out an order form with the manufacturer of souvenirs:

Precise description of service or product

- make certain that they are using the same materials to produce your items as they showed you in the sample
- product number
- catalog page or issue
- whether proofs or examples will be provided
- an assurance of quality to the committee's satisfaction
- shipping and packaging to prevent damage
- specifications sheet from the manufacturer

Dates, places, times

- date of the reunion
- when the order will be placed
- date of delivery
- turnaround time for re-orders

Contact person

- contact name and phone number of the person who took the order

Charges, fees and deposits

- per item costs
- any discounts for quantity
- any interest charges

Methods of payment accepted

- cash, personal or committee check, credit card, billing on account, money order

Payment schedule

- when deposits are due
- when the final payment is due
- whether you can pay in installments
- when deposits will be returned if they are not to be applied to the final bill

Not to exceed clause

- if they plan to produce an overage to cover any products with defects, include a not-to-exceed clause to ensure that you're not paying for extras that you don't want

Extra charges

- fees for direct shipment to your members
- fees for incomplete sets
- design fees
- setup fees
- shipping and handling

Cancellation Policy

- date before which either party can cancel without penalty
- policy for credits and returns
- penalty if they cancel after the designated date
- penalty if you cancel after the designated date

Deadlines or due dates

- date for seeing proofs
- delivery date prior to the reunion
- delivery date to purchasers after the reunion

Deliveries or pickup

- whether the committee will be responsible for picking up the souvenirs or whether they will be delivered
- whether souvenirs will be shipped directly to the purchasers

Shipping method

- USPS, UPS, overnight, insured, registered
- how souvenirs will be packaged to avoid damage
- if damage or loss does occur during shipping, how items will be replaced and how quickly they will be delivered

Staffing or Equipment to be Used

- specify the manufacturing process to be used

Staff's responsibilities

- whether or not they have a backup supplier in case the manufacturer can't deliver in time for the reunion

Committee's responsibilities

- whether the committee will need to provide the company a copy of a logo or camera-ready art prior to production
- who has the authority to increase the number of souvenirs ordered

Non-Performance Penalty

- payment of express charges should items have to be returned before the reunion
- Shipment direct to attendees should souvenirs not arrive in time for the reunion
- if they cancel after the agreed upon non-penalty date, they should pay for any charges that incur in finding another souvenir manufacturer
- if you cancel after the non-penalty date, you should pay only for costs actually incurred
- if merchandise is unsatisfactory or the wrong item is shipped, you may consider witholding payment until delivered and inspected

Chapter 25

Read all About It ... !!! :
The Reunion Book

The souvenir *most* treasured by reunion-goers is a Reunion Book containing information about your members, your group and the reunion. For some groups, a Reunion Book could be a re-creation of a school yearbook, for others it might be a scrapbook, a photo album or a written history. Reunion Books require some effort to design and put together, but you'll be able to tell by the eagerness with which your guests delve into it, that it was worthwhile.

Most Reunion Books include then and now information, photographs, memorabilia and a membership list — a directory, of sorts. Let members write something about themselves and their families. Give them a sheet to fill out and send back to you. This is the easiest way to compile a 'member information' section.

Include memorabilia. A Reunion Book is a terrific way to show it off. Sprinkle it throughout the book or place it all together in a memorabilia section. Include pictures from your last reunion, headlines from an important day in the group's history, illustrations, programs, photographs of nostalgic artifacts, clippings, ticket stubs, movie listings, sports scores, 'On this day in History,' the Oscar winners or Top 40 songs of your year or almanac information. Any memorabilia you've collected could be used in a 'blast from the past' section.

In this chapter you'll find information to help you establish the content, choose a format and title and show you how to get the Reunion Book ready for a book printer.

Reunion Book Trivia Checklist

- ☐ Map of where members live currently
- ☐ How far members will travel to get to the reunion
- ☐ Members' professions
- ☐ Notable achievements
- ☐ Sports scores (championship teams from your group and the pros)
- ☐ Most likely to ... (and whether they did!)
- ☐ Slogans your members would recognize
- ☐ Who belonged to what group (team rosters, club members)

Events that occurred on dates important to the group
- ☐ It happened during _____ (year)
- ☐ It happened on _____ (date)

Events important to your group
- ☐ School (graduation, spring play, homecoming)
- ☐ Family (weddings, births, immigration, pioneers)
- ☐ Military (enlistment, battles fought, returned home)
- ☐ Association (founding date, famous members)
- ☐ Corporate (founding date, important product launch)

Notable quotables
- ☐ Bartlett's Familiar Quotations
- ☐ Bloopers
- ☐ Lines from movies
- ☐ Pundits
- ☐ Entertainers
- ☐ Commercial slogans

Entertainment highlights
- ☐ Most popular movie (what movie was seen the greatest number of times)
- ☐ Most popular song
- ☐ Most popular album
- ☐ Most watched television program

Items familiar to your group
- ☐ Household items
- ☐ Fads
- ☐ Cars driven
- ☐ Clothing styles
- ☐ Items they still have from 'back then'

Places familiar to your group
- ☐ Favorite hangout
- ☐ Favorite gathering place

Reunion Book Budget Matrix

Quantity	Page Count	Unit Cost	Price	Breakeven

Reunion Book Editing Checklist

Check for style consistency

- ☐ Margins
- ☐ Headers
- ☐ Page numbers
- ☐ Borders

Check for typographical errors

Check for completeness

- ☐ Pages in the right order
- ☐ All pages present

Check for electronic submissions problems

- ☐ CMYK colors
- ☐ Binding edge allowance
- ☐ Bleed elements
- ☐ Images within edge boundaries
- ☐ Trim area
- ☐ Line strength
- ☐ Illustrations with blends
- ☐ Reversed out type
- ☐ Nested graphics
- ☐ Electronic white out
- ☐ Halftone scan resolution
- ☐ Lineart scan resolution
- ☐ Images scaled, rotated or cropped
- ☐ Fonts
- ☐ Correct file type
- ☐ Correct file names
- ☐ All files included
- ☐ Color cover proof
- ☐ Laser text proof

Book Printer Interview Checklist

Company Name:		
Address:		
Contact Name:	Phone:	Fax:
E-mail:	URL:	

Printer's experience/specialty

Professional association memberships _____

Binding _____ Short-run _____

Full color _____ Print on demand _____

Printer's fees

Electronic files _____ Plates _____

Halftones _____ Lamination _____

Shrink wrapping _____ Shipping _____

Paper/cover in stock

Printer's equipment specifications

Special services

Typesetting _____ Copywriting _____

Electronic file conversion _____ Cover design _____

Drop shipping _____

Client list/references

Billing Data

Deposit date _____ Deposit amount _____

Deposit date _____ Deposit amount _____

Final payment due _____ Final payment amount _____

Payment methods accepted _____

Signing a Contract with a Book Printer

Consider the following before you fill out an order form or negotiate a contract with a book printer:

Precise description of service or product
- what printing services will be included, how many pieces will be produced
- whether camera-ready artwork will be supplied by the printer
- how the information will be collated
- how the book will be bound
- what cover stock will be used
- how many ink colors will be used
- how many graphics or photographs will be included

Dates, places, times
- date of the reunion
- dates for each meeting with the printer
- dates the art is to be delivered to the printer
- date the proofs to be returned to the committee
- date that the job is to be completed and delivered

Contact person
- contact person and telephone number for the printer
- get an after hours or emergency number

Charges, fees and deposits
- all charges for layout, printing, folding and binding
- whether these charges are by the piece or a flat fee
- whether there are discounts for volume
- what second press run costs are
- whether a deposit is required

Methods of payment accepted
- cash, personal or committee check, credit card, billing on account, money order

Payment schedule
- when deposit is due
- when final payment is due
- when deposits will be returned if they are not applied to the final bill

Not to exceed clause
- if there is a built in overage to cover machine printing mistakes, there should be a dollar amount not to be exceeded for the whole job

Extra charges
- any services not included in the per-book price
- charges for including or producing halftones
- folding, collating, or cutting fees
- setup fees
- artwork placement fees
- charges for making color separations

Cancellation Policy
- cancellation date before which there are no charges
- penalty if you cancel after the no-penalty date
- penalty if the printer cancels after the no-penalty date

Deadlines or due dates
- when books will be delivered

Deliveries or pickup
- whether the committee will be responsible for pickup or whether the printer will ship the books to the committee or directly to the guest list

Shipping method
- USPS, UPS, overnight, registered, insured
- suggest that the printer package books in cartons weighing less than 40 pounds to avoid damage during shipping
- if damage or loss does occur during shipping, how items will be replaced and how quickly they will be delivered

Staffing or Equipment to be Used
- if a specific graphic or printing process will be used then specify the equipment

Staff's responsibilities
- proofreading
- layout design
- photography
- inclusion of graphics
- collation of materials
- making halftones, color separations

Committee's responsibilities
- whether the committee will provide the printer a completed, camera-ready manuscript
- to proof read all copy if the printer is responsible for the typesetting
- providing any or all layouts or artwork
- who has the authority to make changes to the reunion book once the manuscript is in the printer's hands

Non-Performance Penalty
- if the books are not ready for distribution during the reunion, the printer should pay for all packaging and mailing costs for distribution after the reunion
- if the printer cancels after the agreed upon cancellation date, the printer should have to pay for finding another firm to do the job and any rush fees as a result
- if you cancel after the agreed upon date, you should limit yourself to actual expenses incurred to that point

Chapter 26

Multimedia Memoirs:
Making a Reunion CD-ROM

Reunions are perfect opportunities to make the most of multimedia technology. In fact, this is a great project for the 'techies' in your group. Most home computers are now equipped with the means to create incredible multimedia projects. CD-ROM (compact disc recordable) or DVD (digital video disk) are digital storage media with immense capacity to store pictures, graphics and movies. They can be used to create and store multimedia presentations, displays or souvenirs. They're light. They're portable. And, they can be viewed from almost any home computer or DVD player. One of the best features of CD and DVD-ROMs are their storage capacity — 650 to 700 Mb in the case of CDs and more than 4 Gb in the case of DVDs. You don't have to be a multimedia designer to create an impressive CD. Powerful multimedia software will do most of the work.

What exactly can you do with multimedia? Multimedia is used to create everything from electronic books and encyclopedias to fully-interactive video games or training simulations. You may not want to undertake a project as complex as Microsoft's Flight Simulator or Britannica's Encyclopedia but you may want to distribute an electronic version of your Reunion Book or to create a multimedia souvenir.

In this chapter you'll find out how versatile multimedia is. We'll illustrate how multimedia can be used during a reunion and give you some multimedia design wisdom to help you create your multimedia project.

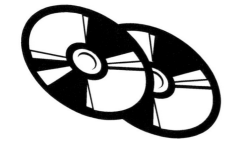

Multimedia Design Checklist

Software
- [ ] Multimedia authoring
- [ ] Presentation
- [ ] Web design
- [ ] Video editing
- [ ] Animation
- [ ] Electronic book
- [ ] Multimedia photo albums
- [ ] Image editing
- [ ] Audio editing

Page Design
- [ ] Launch page
- [ ] Design for a horizontal screen
- [ ] Consistent design style
- [ ] Type big enough to read
- [ ] Consistent alignment
- [ ] Non-busy backgrounds
- [ ] Pages not too busy
- [ ] Design within the usable area
- [ ] Consistent type styles
- [ ] Use fancy type sparingly
- [ ] Correct proximity

Navigation Design
- [ ] Disk map
- [ ] Exit
- [ ] Links that look like links
- [ ] Linear navigation
- [ ] Hierarchical navigation
- [ ] Visual/audio indicator
- [ ] Help
- [ ] Common elements on every page
- [ ] Buttons that look like buttons
- [ ] Menu navigation
- [ ] Network navigation

Integration
- [ ] Consistent naming convention
- [ ] No characters in the file name
- [ ] Defragment the hard drive
      before creating the master
- [ ] 8 character file names + extension
- [ ] Simple folder levels

Testing
- [ ] User testing
- [ ] Functional testing
- [ ] Interface testing

Product Packaging
- [ ] Label case
- [ ] Documentation
- [ ] Package insert

Multimedia Disk Map Storyboard

Opening Graphic

Multimedia Designer Interview Checklist

Company Name:		
Address:		
Contact Name:	Phone:	Fax:
E-mail:	URL:	

Multimedia designer's experience

Professional association memberships _____

Portfolio _____ Linear projects _____

Interactive Projects _____ E-books _____

Design fees

Design/re-design _____ Testing _____

Master _____ Duplication _____

Design criteria

Project approval process

Extra services

Scans _____ Video editing/conversion _____

Package design _____ Instructions _____

Duplication

Client list/references

Billing Data

Deposit date _____ Deposit amount _____

Deposit date _____ Deposit amount _____

Final payment due _____ Final payment amount _____

Payment methods accepted _____

Signing a Contract with a Multimedia Designer

Consider the following before you negotiate a contract with a multimedia designer:

Precise description of service or product

- exactly what the disk will include, how many sections, how many pages, how many images, etc.
- whether the multimedia designer will create original graphics or use Clip Art
- which software the disk will be developed with
- all troubleshooting (broken links, missing graphics, unacceptable pages) will be fixed without charge
- Design for product packaging
- Documentation for the disk

Dates, places, times

- date of the reunion
- dates for each meeting with the multimedia designer
- dates the initial disk design will be completed
- date the approved design will be available for demonstration
- date the final disks must be available for distribution

Contact person

- contact person and telephone number for the multimedia designer
- after hours or emergency number

Charges, fees and deposits

- all charges for design, scanning, graphics
- whether these charges are hourly or a flat fee
- whether a deposit is required

Methods of payment accepted

- cash, personal or committee check, credit card, billing on account, money order

Payment schedule

- when deposit is due
- when incremental and final payments are due
- when deposits will be returned if they are not applied to the final bill

Not to exceed clause

- if charges will be hourly, you might want to include a not to exceed clause for the design

Extra charges

- any services not included in the disk design fee
- charges for scanning or preparing photographs
- charges for creating original graphics
- charges for altering your electronic files

Cancellation Policy

- cancellation date before which there are no charges
- penalty if you cancel after the no-penalty date
- penalty if the web designer cancels after the no-penalty date

Deadlines or due dates

- when the initial design will be ready for your approval
- when the disk will be tested
- when master disk will be ready for your approval
- when the disk must go to the duplication house

Deliveries or pickup

- whether the multimedia designer will ship or deliver a demonstration version to the committee for approval

Shipping method

- USPS, UPS, overnight, registered, insured, FTP, download, e-mail

Software or Equipment to be Used

- if a specific multimedia authorizing software is to be used to create the disk so that it can be read on multiple platforms, specify the software

Staff's responsibilities

- disk and graphic design
- inclusion and development of visual images
- proofreading
- troubleshooting the disk

Committee's responsibilities

- whether the committee will provide any electronic images to be used for the disk
- to evaluate the disk and give final approval before the master is sent to the duplication house

Non-Performance Penalty

- if the disk is not ready for distribution by the agreed upon date, the designer should reduce the design fee
- if the designer cancels after the agreed upon cancellation date, the designer should have to pay for finding another multimedia designer to do the job and any rush fees as a result
- if you cancel after the agreed upon date, you should limit yourself to actual work completed at that point

Multimedia Duplication House Interview Checklist

Company Name:	
Address:	
Contact Name:	Phone: Fax:
E-mail:	URL:

Duplication fees

Additional services

File preparation rules

Turn around time

Returns policy

Client list/references

Billing Data

Deposit date _____ Deposit amount_____

Deposit date _____ Deposit amount_____

Final payment due _____ Final payment amount_____

Payment methods accepted _____

Signing a Contract with a Duplication House

Consider the following before you negotiate a contract with a duplication house:

Precise description of service or product
- how much disk space your material will require
- what software is supported and how you will provide the files
- how many disks will be created
- how the disks will be checked for defects
- how the disks will be labeled and packaged

Dates, places, times
- date the master disk will arrive at the duplication house
- date the duplicates should be delivered

Contact person
- contact person and telephone number for the duplication house
- get an after hours or emergency number in case the disks are not delivered on time

Charges, fees and deposits
- all duplication fees and setup charges
- whether there are fees for files conversion
- fees for product packaging
- fees for labeling or imprinting the disks
- whether a deposit is required

Methods of payment accepted
- cash, personal or committee check, credit card, billing on account, money order

Payment schedule
- when (if) deposit is due
- when final payment is due

Extra charges
- charges to function test the disk
- charges to drop ship directly to buyers
- charges to print documentation and case inserts
- charges for mailing packages

Cancellation Policy
- cancellation date before which there are no charges
- penalty if you cancel after the no-penalty date
- penalty if the printer cancels after the no-penalty date

Deadlines or due dates
- when the disks must be available for buyers

Deliveries or pickup
- if any files or demonstration disks must be sent, how they will be delivered and packaged to prevent damage

Shipping method
- USPS, UPS, overnight, registered, insured, FTP, download

Staffing or Equipment to be Used
- what equipment will be used to create the disks
- what printing equipment will be used to imprint or label the disks
- what printing equipment will be used to create documentation and package inserts

Staff's responsibilities
- testing the master disk
- testing the duplicated disks

Committee's responsibilities
- to provide the duplication house with correct electronic and graphics files

Non-Performance Penalty
- if the disks are not available for distribution, the duplication house should pay to have the disks delivered directly to the buyers

Chapter 27

Lights, Camera, Action!!!: Making a Reunion Video

ideo captures a memory. It holds on to a slice of time and records it with pictures and sound as a lasting record of the festivities. Because each reunion is a one-time occasion, making a video is a way to capture the essence of each event as it's happening, as well as a way to record your memorabilia and other displays. Your video could be a souvenir or it could be used for a presentation. Producing a video is not as hard as you might think. In fact, you may have the next Steven Spielberg in your midst. More and more, video is being used to record reunion events in addition to still photography.

Why shouldn't you just show up and shoot? Because producing a video takes some preparation and planning in order to get a good final product. Start with a plan. You can't get a good video out of lousy footage. Unedited video of a bunch of people in a ballroom is like watching a security camera. Hours and hours of 'live action' video makes for a very boring video. Edit out the dull stuff. That's not to say you shouldn't take video while you're in the midst of the reunion. You should, but you'll want additional footage to intersperse with live action shots for a more exciting final video.

In this chapter you'll find information to help you choose a format for the video, suggest tips for shooting and editing, preserve your video for future reunions or for future generations to enjoy. Should you need help from a professional, we'll give you tips for working with a videographer.

Video Preparation Checklist

Preparation

- [ ] Storyboard
- [ ] Shotsheet
- [ ] Script
- [ ] Spotter
- [ ] Site Inspection
- [ ] Talent

Equipment

- [ ] Videocamera
- [ ] Videotape
- [ ] Batteries
- [ ] Lighting
- [ ] Tripod
- [ ] Microphones
- [ ] Backdrops
- [ ] Backup equipment

Software

- [ ] Video editing
- [ ] Audio editing
- [ ] Image editing

Site Inspection

- [ ] Weather
- [ ] Space/clutter
- [ ] Background colors
- [ ] Background noise
- [ ] Lighting conditions
- [ ] Available power sources
- [ ] Local audio feeds
- [ ] Test video
- [ ] Test audio
- [ ] On-site photographs

Title Ideas

- [ ] Letters in icing
- [ ] Rub-on lettering
- [ ] Color art board
- [ ] Index cards
- [ ] Stencils
- [ ] Clear plastic gels
- [ ] Confetti
- [ ] Colored sidewalk chalk
- [ ] Titles on plexiglass
- [ ] Scrolls
- [ ] Postcards
- [ ] Lite Bright™

Video Storyboard

Video description	Audio description	Script

Video 1	
Video 2	
Audio 1	
Audio 2	
Titles	
Transitions	

Video description	Audio description	Script

Video 1	
Video 2	
Audio 1	
Audio 2	
Titles	
Transitions	

Video Shotsheet

Video wanted	Time occurring	Place occurring

Videographer Interview Checklist

Company Name:

Address:

Contact Name: Phone: Fax:

E-mail: URL:

Videographer's experience

Corporate events _____ Anniversary _____

Weddings _____ Professional association memberships _____

Videographer's portfolio

Camera angles _____ Composition _____

Editing _____ Special effects _____

Personnel

Number _____

Attire _____

Equipment

Backup equipment _____

Fees

Special services

Duplication _____

Copyrights

Backup plans

Client list/references

Billing Data

Deposit date _____ Deposit amount _____

Deposit date _____ Deposit amount _____

Final payment due _____ Final payment amount _____

Payment methods accepted _____

Signing a Contract with a Videographer

Consider the following before you negotiate a contract with a videographer:

Precise description of service or product

- the editing process
- the vision for the final product
- special effects used
- approximate final length
- any special services such as shipping and packaging
- contingency plans
- extra services such as: lighting, storage of the final video, etc.
- who owns the roughcut video as well as reproduction and duplication rights
- whether you will allow the videographer to use your tape as a part of their portfolio
- how the tapes will be duplicated
- whether a copy will be kept in permanent storage

Dates, places, times

- date and location of the reunion
- start and end times of each event
- dates, places and times for meetings, site check, filming, and editing
- when the videographer will arrive and how long they will stay

Contact person

- the contact person and phone number for the firm
- the name and phone number of the actual videographer
- get an after hours or emergency number

Charges, fees, and deposits

- whether there will be a guaranteed purchase
- fees for each service
- deposits
- any discounts that apply

Methods of payment accepted

- cash, personal or committee check, credit card, billing on account, money order

Payment schedule

- when deposits are due
- payments in installments
- when final payment is due
- interest (if charged)
- when deposit is returned if not applied to the final bill

Not to exceed clause

- especially if you are using an hourly rate, you may want to include a not to exceed clause

Extra charges

- props, extra equipment or staff, shipping, storage, special effects, music, equipment purchase or rental

Cancellation Policy

- no penalties if you cancel before a specified date
- if you cancel, payment of actual expenses incurred only
- if they cancel, payment of expenses incurred in finding another videographer

Deadlines or due dates

- when videos will be available for distribution

Deliveries or pickup

- whether the committee will pick up the tapes or whether they will be shipped to the committee or directly to the purchasers

Shipping method

- If the information is to be shipped to you, by which method -- USPS, UPS, registered, insured, overnight
- how the video will be boxed and protected for mailing
- if damage or loss does occur during shipping, how items will be replaced and how quickly they will be delivered

Staffing or Equipment to be Used

- who will be in charge of filming
- who will be in charge of editing
- any extra personnel who will be in attendance
- the conduct and dress of the videographers
- how many cameras will be present
- whether lighting will be supplied
- who will supply props or backdrops
- backup plans

Staff's responsibilities

- storyboarding
- concept development
- site inspection and preparation
- directing the shoot
- editing
- special effects
- coaching actors

Committee's responsibilities

- what the committee will provide to the videographer (suggested shots, graphics)
- when the committee will be available for viewing prior to editing

Non-Performance Penalty

- a discount in final payment should the quality of the final tape not meet committee's expectations
- covering the cost of hiring someone at the last minute in case of a no-show

Video Duplication House Interview Checklist

Company Name:	
Address:	
Contact Name:	Phone: Fax:
E-mail:	URL:

Duplication fees

Additional services

File submission rules

Turnaround time

Returns policy

Client list/references

Billing Data

Deposit date _____ Deposit amount_____

Deposit date _____ Deposit amount_____

Final payment due _____ Final payment amount_____

Payment methods accepted _____

Signing a Contract with a Video Duplication House

Consider the following before you negotiate a contract with a video duplication house:

Precise description of service or product
- how much time you'll have on the final tape
- what video types are supported and how you will provide the originals
- how many videos will be created
- how the videos will be checked for defects
- how the videos will be packaged

Dates, places, times
- date the master video will arrive at the duplication house
- date the duplicates should be delivered

Contact person
- contact person and telephone number for the duplication house
- get an after hours or emergency number in case the videos are not delivered on time

Charges, fees and deposits
- all duplication fees and setup charges
- whether there are fees for video type conversion
- fees for product packaging
- fees for labeling the videos
- fees for slip covers for videos
- whether a deposit is required

Methods of payment accepted
- cash, personal or committee check, credit card, billing on account, money order

Payment schedule
- when (if) deposit is due
- when monthly payments are due

Extra charges
- charges to preview the video
- charges to drop ship directly to buyers
- charges to print labels and cases
- charges for mailing packages

Cancellation Policy
- cancellation date before which there are no charges
- penalty if you cancel after the no-penalty date
- penalty if the printer cancels after the no-penalty date

Deadlines or due dates
- when the videos must be available for buyers

Deliveries or pickup
- how the master video will be sent and packaged to prevent damage

Shipping method
- USPS, UPS, overnight, registered, insured, FTP, download

Staffing or Equipment to be Used
- what equipment will be used to create the videos
- what printing equipment will be used to imprint or label the videos

Staff's responsibilities
- testing the master video
- testing the duplicated videos

Committee's responsibilities
- to provide the duplication house with appropriate video and graphics files for labels and packaging

Non-Performance Penalty
- if the videos are not available for distribution, the duplication house should pay to have the videos delivered directly to the buyers

Chapter 28

Snapshots:
Photography

Photographs are lasting reminders of a memorable event. Photographs let us record a moment, to sense and capture life as it happens. Photographs make beautiful decorations, money-making souvenirs and are much appreciated by guests who forget their own cameras or who just don't have a knack for capturing good pictures. The trick is not just to know how to take a photograph, but what to photograph.

Use photographs to capture the essence of the reunion. Get a good photograph of the entire group. Shoot candids during each event. Get snapshots of the setup and the memorabilia. Take some formal portraits or capture the little moments that are meaningful.

Preparation isn't quite as crucial with still photography as it is with videography, but there are a few things that you'll want do before you photograph your reunion. The more prepared you are, the better pictures you'll take.

In this chapter you'll find information to help you determine what type of photographs will best capture your celebration, suggest tips for shooting, determine what equipment you'll need, suggest ways to use photographs throughout the reunion and show you how to create photo souvenirs. If you can't find someone within your group who can take a good photograph, we'll give you tips for hiring a photographer.

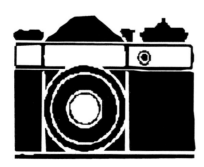

Photography Preparation Checklist

Site inspection
- [ ] Lighting
- [ ] Time of day
- [ ] Distance from subject

Equipment
- [ ] Camera
- [ ] Film/disk/memory stick
- [ ] Batteries
- [ ] Lighting
- [ ] Tripod
- [ ] Shot sheet
- [ ] Spotter
- [ ] Log sheet
- [ ] Backup equipment

Photo Editing
- [ ] Scanner
- [ ] Image editing software
- [ ] Photo restoration software

Shot Ideas
- [ ] Candids
- [ ] Establishing shots
- [ ] Portraits
- [ ] Group shots
- [ ] B&Ws

Site Inspection
- [ ] Weather
- [ ] Space/clutter
- [ ] Backgrounds
- [ ] Space for theme backgrounds
- [ ] Lighting conditions
- [ ] On-site photographs

Photography Shot Sheet

Photograph wanted	Time occurring	Place occurring

Photographer Interview Checklist

Company Name:

Address:

Contact Name: Phone: Fax:

E-mail: URL:

Photographer's experience

Professional association memberships_____

Portraits_____ Landscapes_____ Candids_____

Group photographs_____ B&Ws_____ Children_____

Photographer's portfolio

Personnel

Number_____

Attire _____

Equipment

Backup equipment _____

Fees

Special services

Albums_____ Duplication _____

Contact sheets_____ Full size proofs _____

Copyrights

Backup plans

Client list/references

Billing Data

    Deposit date _____ Deposit amount_____

    Deposit date _____ Deposit amount_____

    Final payment due _____ Final payment amount_____

    Payment methods accepted _____

Signing a Contract with a Photographer

Consider the following before you negotiate a contract with a photographer:

Precise description of service or product

- exactly what and who the photographer is to shoot
- how long the photographer will stay at each event
- the size of proofs and reprints
- minimum number of shots taken
- copyrights (reprint rights, reproduction rights)
- whether negatives will be kept in permanent storage
- special effects used (e.g. captioning)
- any special services such as shipping and packaging
- contingency plans
- whether photographs will be mounted, framed or gathered in albums
- whether the photographer will provide backgrounds, captions, event identifiers, lighting, special effects

Dates, places, times

- date and location of the reunion
- start and end times of each event
- what time the photographer will arrive and how long they will stay
- where, what time and day the committee will meet with the photographer to go over the shot sheet prior to the reunion

Contact person

- contact person and phone number for the firm
- name and phone number for the actual photographer who will be working with you
- get an after hours or emergency number

Charges, fees, and deposits

- whether there will be a guaranteed purchase, fees for each service
- deposits
- what any package prices include (e.g., number of exposures, proofs, prints, etc.)
- hourly rate
- any discounts that apply

Methods of payment accepted

- personal or committee checks, billing on account, credit cards, money order, cash

Payment schedule

- when deposits are due
- payments in installments
- when final payment is due
- interest (if charged)
- when deposit is returned if not applied to the final bill

Not to exceed clause

- if you are paying by the frame shot, you may want to limit the number (overall or per event)

Extra charges

- albums
- travel time or overtime
- extra equipment or personnel
- oversized prints, panoramic shots

Cancellation Policy

- if you cancel, payment of actual expenses incurred only
- no penalties if you cancel before a specified date
- if they cancel, payment of expenses incurred in finding another investigator

Deadlines or due dates

- when pictures will be available for viewing (during the reunion), sale or distribution
- when reprints or albums will be delivered
- the turnaround time for the proofs

Deliveries or pickup

- whether the committee will pick up the pictures or whether they will be shipped directly to the committee or to the buyers

Shipping method

- If the photographs are to be shipped to you, by which method — USPS, UPS, registered, insured, overnight
- if damage or loss does occur during shipping, how items will be replaced and how quickly they will be delivered

Staffing or Equipment to be Used

- how many cameras will be present
- whether lighting will be supplied
- the size of the film (35mm, 4x5, etc.)
- the quality of reproductions

Staff's responsibilities

- who will be in charge of taking photographs
- any extra personnel who will be in attendance
- the conduct and dress of the photographers

Committee's responsibilities

- what the committee will provide to the photographer (suggested shots, graphics, backdrops)
- when the committee will be available for proofing
- who has the authority to extend the time the photographer stays or the number of exposures taken

Non-Performance Penalty

- a discount in final payment should the quality of the photographs not meet committee's expectations
- there should be a provision covering the cost of hiring someone at the last minute in case of a no-show

Chapter 29

See It To Believe It:
Putting All the Pieces Together

You're in the home stretch — the last 60 days before the reunion. Why are these last eight weeks so important? Because it's time for the committee to really get in gear. It's a high-energy time with lots of excitement. It's the time period between the deadline we suggested for registration and payment and the reunion. After you pass the payment deadline, it's time to evaluate where you are — whether you met your target attendance number, how you're doing financially and what remains to be done before the reunion. If everything is right on schedule, you can clear the decks of any remaining tasks and get ready for the reunion. If you're not exactly where you thought you would be, it's time to create some contingency plans.

This is the time to be ultra-organized because you'll be busy and good pre-planning will help make the reunion run smoothly. At this point, the interdependence of committee jobs will become very apparent. Remember to leave enough time for yourselves. Get as much done as early as possible so that the last couple of weeks won't turn into a scramble to get everything done.

In this chapter you'll find information to help you evaluate your financial status, take a snapshot of committee tasks, develop a timeline for each reunion event, conduct a facility walk-through, develop policies and contingency plans, set up an efficient check-in and registration system and handle volunteers.

Budget Check

Target Attendance Number _____

Per-Person Breakeven Cost _____

Expected Revenue

      Number of couples _____ at $ _____

      Number or singles _____ at $ _____

      A la carte total   _____

TOTAL revenue expected   _____

Current Attendance Number _____

Current Revenue

      Number of couples _____ at $ _____

      Number of singles _____ at $ _____

      A la carte total   _____

TOTAL revenue collected to date   _____

Per-Person Breakeven cost _____ x attendance number _____ = _____

Profit/Loss   _____

Raising revenues	Cutting costs

Last 8 Weeks
Task Sheet

8	7	6	5
4	3	2	1

Check Current Week

Task Description	
Deadline	
Committee Action Needed	
Volunteers Needed	
Name	Phone
Name	Phone
Name	Phone
Name	Phone
Name	Phone

Task Description	
Deadline	
Committee Action Needed	
Volunteers Needed	
Name	Phone
Name	Phone
Name	Phone
Name	Phone
Name	Phone

Task Description	
Deadline	
Committee Action Needed	
Volunteers Needed	
Name	Phone
Name	Phone
Name	Phone
Name	Phone
Name	Phone

Task Description	
Deadline	
Committee Action Needed	
Volunteers Needed	
Name	Phone
Name	Phone
Name	Phone
Name	Phone
Name	Phone

Task Description	
Deadline	
Committee Action Needed	
Subcommittee Action Needed	
Subcommittee Members for This Task	
Name	Phone
Name	Phone
Name	Phone
Name	Phone
Name	Phone

Task Description	
Deadline	
Committee Action Needed	
Subcommittee Action Needed	
Subcommittee Members for This Task	
Name	Phone
Name	Phone
Name	Phone
Name	Phone
Name	Phone

Task Description	
Deadline	
Committee Action Needed	
Subcommittee Action Needed	
Subcommittee Members for This Task	
Name	Phone
Name	Phone
Name	Phone
Name	Phone
Name	Phone

Task Description	
Deadline	
Committee Action Needed	
Subcommittee Action Needed	
Subcommittee Members for This Task	
Name	Phone
Name	Phone
Name	Phone
Name	Phone
Name	Phone

Committee Task Tracker — The Last 8 Weeks

Meeting date	Meeting place

Weeks left before the reunion

Meeting goals summary

Accountant

Record Keeper

Communications Czar

Event Chairman

Event Chairman

Event Chairman

Event Chairman

Executive Committee Chairman

Amenities Coordinator

CD-ROM Coordinator

Decorations Coordinator

Fund-raising Coordinator

Member Search Coordinator

Memorabilia Coordinator

Memorials Coordinator

Music Coordinator

Presentation Coordinator

Photography Coordinator

Reunion Book Coordinator

Souvenirs Coordinator

Videography Coordinator

Volunteer Coordinator

Website Coordinator

Setup Timeline Checklist

Time	Task	Supplies	Assigned to
Time	Task	Supplies	Assigned to
Time	Task	Supplies	Assigned to
Time	Task	Supplies	Assigned to
Time	Task	Supplies	Assigned to
Time	Task	Supplies	Assigned to
Time	Task	Supplies	Assigned to
Time	Task	Supplies	Assigned to
Time	Task	Supplies	Assigned to
Time	Task	Supplies	Assigned to
Time	Task	Supplies	Assigned to
Time	Task	Supplies	Assigned to
Time	Task	Supplies	Assigned to
Time	Task	Supplies	Assigned to
Time	Task	Supplies	Assigned to

Cleanup Timeline Checklist

Do not throw away items

Time	Task	Supplies	Assigned to
Time	Task	Supplies	Assigned to
Time	Task	Supplies	Assigned to
Time	Task	Supplies	Assigned to
Time	Task	Supplies	Assigned to
Time	Task	Supplies	Assigned to
Time	Task	Supplies	Assigned to
Time	Task	Supplies	Assigned to
Time	Task	Supplies	Assigned to
Time	Task	Supplies	Assigned to
Time	Task	Supplies	Assigned to
Time	Task	Supplies	Assigned to
Time	Task	Supplies	Assigned to
Time	Task	Supplies	Assigned to

Event Timeline Checklist

Begin Time	End time	Signal to begin	Assigned to
Begin Time	End time	Signal to begin	Assigned to
Begin Time	End time	Signal to begin	Assigned to
Begin Time	End time	Signal to begin	Assigned to
Begin Time	End time	Signal to begin	Assigned to
Begin Time	End time	Signal to begin	Assigned to
Begin Time	End time	Signal to begin	Assigned to
Begin Time	End time	Signal to begin	Assigned to
Begin Time	End time	Signal to begin	Assigned to
Begin Time	End time	Signal to begin	Assigned to
Begin Time	End time	Signal to begin	Assigned to
Begin Time	End time	Signal to begin	Assigned to
Begin Time	End time	Signal to begin	Assigned to
Begin Time	End time	Signal to begin	Assigned to
Begin Time	End time	Signal to begin	Assigned to

Event Timeline Checklist

Begin Time	End time	Signal to begin	Assigned to
Begin Time	End time	Signal to begin	Assigned to
Begin Time	End time	Signal to begin	Assigned to
Begin Time	End time	Signal to begin	Assigned to
Begin Time	End time	Signal to begin	Assigned to
Begin Time	End time	Signal to begin	Assigned to
Begin Time	End time	Signal to begin	Assigned to
Begin Time	End time	Signal to begin	Assigned to
Begin Time	End time	Signal to begin	Assigned to
Begin Time	End time	Signal to begin	Assigned to
Begin Time	End time	Signal to begin	Assigned to
Begin Time	End time	Signal to begin	Assigned to
Begin Time	End time	Signal to begin	Assigned to
Begin Time	End time	Signal to begin	Assigned to
Begin Time	End time	Signal to begin	Assigned to
Begin Time	End time	Signal to begin	Assigned to

Facility Walk-Through Checklist

Date:	Facility:	Event Start	Event End

Event Description:

Timeline for Events:

8:00			
9:00			
10:00			
11:00			
Noon			
1:00			
2:00			
3:00			
4:00			
5:00			
6:00			
7:00			
8:00			
9:00			
10:00			
11:00			
Midnight			

Facility sketch

Facility Walk-Through Checklist

Room Floor Plan

Registration Kit Checklist

- [ ] Bags
- [ ] Nametags
- [ ] Reunion book
- [ ] Announcements/reminders
- [ ] Schedule of events
- [ ] Local attractions information
- [ ] Maps
- [ ] Missing list
- [ ] Souvenir order forms
- [ ] Medical emergencies information
- [ ] Committee list

- [ ] Labels
- [ ] Event rickets
- [ ] Souvenirs/giveaways
- [ ] Updates
- [ ] Facility(ies) information
- [ ] Tourist information
- [ ] General information sheet
- [ ] Stay in touch information
- [ ] Contest entry forms/rules
- [ ] Evaluations
- [ ] Vendor/sponsors list

Registration Area Sketch

Facility Walk-Through Checklist

Facility Amenities

Entrances _____

Handicap accessible entrances _____

Exits _____

Restrooms _____

Elevators _____

Handicap accessible elevators _____

Freight elevators _____

Front desk services _____

Concierge services _____

Doorman services _____

Bellman services _____

Security services - inside _____

Security services - outside _____

Guest rooms _____

Hospitality suite _____

Recreation facilities _____ Cost _____ Hours _____

Parking _____ Cost _____ Hours _____

Valet Parking _____ Cost _____ Hours _____

Cleaner _____ Cost _____ Hours _____

Babysitting _____ Cost _____ Hours _____

Restaurant _____ Price range _____ Hours _____

Room Service _____ Price range _____ Hours _____

Gift shop _____ Hours _____

Check cashing _____ Fees _____ Hours _____

ATMs _____

Nearby restaurants _____

Nearby services _____

Emergency facilities _____

Local emergency number _____

Outside the facility

Appearance _____

Services available _____

Signs needed _____

Staff needed _____

Facility Walk-Through Checklist

Entrance

Appearance_____

Services available_____

Signs needed_____

Staff needed_____

Lobby

Marquee_____ Sign frames_____

Sign stands_____ Glass sign cases_____

Coat check _____

Other services available_____

Staff needed_____

Initial Room Check

Entrances_____

Exits_____

Fire extinguishers_____

Overhead music controls_____

Light switches_____

Air/Heat controls_____

Outlets_____

Vendors Meeting

Catering

    Space needed_____

    Time for setup_____

    Time for breakdown_____

    Signs needed_____

    Staff needed_____

Beverage service

    Space needed_____

    Time for setup_____

    Time for breakdown_____

    Signs needed_____

    Staff needed_____

    _____

    _____

Facility Walk-Through Checklist

Vendors Meeting, cont.

Security

    Space needed _____

    Time for setup _____

    Time for breakdown _____

    Signs needed _____

    Staff needed _____

Parking

    Space needed _____

    Time for setup _____

    Time for breakdown _____

    Signs needed _____

    Staff needed _____

Doorman

    Space needed _____

    Time for setup _____

    Time for breakdown _____

    Signs needed _____

    Staff needed _____

Audio-Visual services

    Space needed _____

    Time for setup _____

    Time for breakdown _____

    Signs needed _____

    Staff needed _____

Photographer

    Space needed _____

    Time for setup _____

    Time for breakdown _____

    Signs needed _____

    Staff needed _____

Videographer

    Space needed _____

    Time for setup _____

    Time for breakdown _____

    Signs needed _____

    Staff needed _____

Facility Walk-Through Checklist

Committee Meeting

Decorations Coordinator

Space needed _____

Time for setup _____

Time for breakdown _____

Signs needed _____

Staff needed _____

Souvenirs Coordinator

Space needed _____

Time for setup _____

Time for breakdown _____

Signs needed _____

Staff needed _____

Memorabilia Coordinator

Space needed _____

Time for setup _____

Time for breakdown _____

Signs needed _____

Staff needed _____

Memorials Coordinator

Space needed _____

Time for setup _____

Time for breakdown _____

Signs needed _____

Staff needed _____

Presentations Coordinator

Space needed _____

Time for setup _____

Time for breakdown _____

Signs needed _____

Staff needed _____

Facility Walk-Through Checklist

Music Coordinator

Space needed _____

Time for setup _____

Time for breakdown _____

Signs needed _____

Staff needed _____

Reunion Book Coordinator

Space needed _____

Time for setup _____

Time for breakdown _____

Signs needed _____

Staff needed _____

CD-ROM Coordinator

Space needed _____

Time for setup _____

Time for breakdown _____

Signs needed _____

Staff needed _____

Videography Coordinator

Space needed _____

Time for setup _____

Time for breakdown _____

Signs needed _____

Staff needed _____

Photography Coordinator

Space needed _____

Time for setup _____

Time for breakdown _____

Signs needed _____

Staff needed _____

Equipment Check

Sound system _____   Microphones _____

Lighting _____   AV Equipment _____

Monitors _____   Electricity needs _____

Extra power strips needed _____

Extension cords needed _____

Chapter 30

Here at Last:
At the Reunion

The end is in sight. Soon, all your hard work will come to fruition. There are still a few things to do before you can sit back and enjoy the party including taking steps to ensure that committee members aren't so busy that they can't enjoy their own reunion.

Because committee members and their representatives (professional planners, service providers or staff at the registration desk) will be highly visible, naturally they will be the people to whom guests will turn with complaints or praise. You can help the committee, staff and volunteers to respond in a consistent way by anticipating the situations they might face.

As a committee, get ready to be good hosts. If you're creating a Reunion Book using updated member information, make photocopies of submissions and let the committee read them. If you see anyone looking ill at ease, help guests to become reacquainted with each other. Help the introductions along. Suggest other members or their spouses to talk to. Make it easier for guests to strike up conversations with each other. Spouses are often left as an afterthought at reunions. Help spouses who might not know anyone at the reunion to meet other guests in the same profession or who have the same hobbies. Do anything you can do to make *all* guests feel welcome.

In this chapter you'll find information to help you implement the pre-planning you undertook in Chapter 29 — preparing the committee for what will take place during the reunion, coordinating each event, settling the bills and cleaning up.

Committee Preparation Sheet

Committee Preparation

Vision statement _____
_____
Reunion book submissions/yearbook/family history _____

Committee expectations for the reunion

Information sheets
    FAQs _____   Reunion information sheet_____
    Schedule of events _____   Vendors list_____
    Site maps_____   Committee list_____
    Vendor/sponsors list _____

Answers to common questions
    What prices include_____   Cost comparison sheet_____
    Reunion costs _____   Plans for the money_____
    What was done to locate members_____   Who is still on the missing list_____

Policies
    Alcohol_____   Payment_____
    Refund_____   Pricing_____
    Ticket system_____   Reconciliation_____
    Lost tickets_____

Answers to objections or complaints

At the Reunion Checklist

Date:	Facility:	Event Start	Event End

Event Description:

Timeline for Events:

8:00			
9:00			
10:00			
11:00			
Noon			
1:00			
2:00			
3:00			
4:00			
5:00			
6:00			
7:00			
8:00			
9:00			
10:00			
11:00			
Midnight			

Facility Contact Information:

Facility manager_____ Phone number_____

Event manager_____ Phone number_____

Catering manager_____ Phone number_____

Housekeeping _____ Phone number_____

Building maintenance _____ Phone number_____

AV/Technical assistance _____ Phone number_____

Parking _____ Phone number_____

Security _____ Phone number_____

Concierge _____ Phone number_____

Cab companies:

Name _____ Phone number_____

Name _____ Phone number_____

Name _____ Phone number_____

Name _____ Phone number_____

Emergency numbers: (not all areas use 911)

Fire _____ Phone number_____

Police _____ Phone number_____

Ambulance_____ Phone number_____

Hospitals _____ Phone number_____

At the Reunion Checklist

Vendor's List:

Executive Committee Chairman	
Vendor	Description
Event Chairman	
Vendor	Description
Vendor	Description
Vendor	Description
Vendor	Description
Vendor	Description
Vendor	Description
Amenities Coordinator	
Vendor	Description
Vendor	Description
Vendor	Description
CD-ROM Coordinator	
Vendor	Description
Decorations Coordinator	
Vendor	Description
Vendor	Description
Vendor	Description
Fund-raising Coordinator	
Vendor	Description
Memorabilia Coordinator	
Vendor	Description
Memorials Coordinator	
Vendor	Description
Music Coordinator	
Vendor	Description
Presentation Coordinator	
Vendor	Description
Vendor	Description
Vendor	Description
Photography Coordinator	
Vendor	Description
Reunion Book Coordinator	
Vendor	Description
Souvenirs Coordinator	
Vendor	Description
Videography Coordinator	
Vendor	Description
Volunteer Coordinator	
Vendor	Description
Vendor	Description

At the Reunion Checklist

Facility:

Area Sketch

At the Reunion Checklist

Facility:

Room Setup Sketch

Food Service Tables Setup

Catering Service _____ Catering contact_____

Setup area_____ Committee contact _____

Setup time_____ Breakdown time_____

Beverage Service Setup

Beverage Service _____ Beverage contact_____

Setup area_____ Committee contact _____

Setup time_____ Breakdown time_____

At the Reunion Checklist

Entrance:

Appearance_____ Doorman _____

Facility site map_____

Signs_____

Lobby:

Appearance_____ Concierge _____

Front Desk Staff_____ Coat check _____

Signs_____

Registration Area:

Traffic Flow_____ Expected Peak Traffic _____

Express line_____ Walk-up line_____

Personnel

     Name_____ Shift _____

     Name_____ Shift _____

     Name_____ Shift _____

     Name_____ Shift _____

     Name_____ Shift _____

     Name_____ Shift _____

     Name_____ Shift _____

     Name_____ Shift _____

Activities _____

Signs_____

Registration Table:

Instructions/Training Materials_____ Attendee list _____

Tables_____ Chairs _____

Tickets_____ Order forms _____

Office supplies _____ Cash Box/Cash_____

Staff nametags _____ Guest nametags_____

Souvenirs _____ Souvenir sales information _____

Site maps_____ Shade _____

Bottled water_____ Cell phones/walkie-talkies_____

Signs_____

At the Reunion Checklist

Training Materials:

Vision statement_____ Committee list_____

Facility contact list_____ Reunion information sheet_____

Attendee list_____ Special guest list_____

Synopsis of roles and responsibilities_____ Personnel assignment sheet_____

Frequently asked questions sheet_____ Emergency contact information sheet_____

Policy sheets

        Alcohol _____ Refunds_____

        Payment _____ Pricing_____

        Ticket system _____ Reconciliation system_____

Practice forms_____ Site maps_____

Registration Desk Supplies List:

Note pads _____ Paper clips_____

Stapler/staples_____ Box cutter_____

Tape (transparent, masking, electrical, duct, packing) _____

Pens/pencils _____ Clip boards_____

Flashlight_____ Leatherman tool _____

Hammer_____ Screwdriver_____

First-aid kit _____ Extension cords_____

Extra batteries_____ Clamps_____

Ziploc bags_____ Garbage bags_____

Insect repellant_____ Sunscreen_____

Tarps_____ Ponchos_____

Bullhorn _____ Fire extinguisher_____

Walk-in Registration Supplies List:

Blank nametags _____ Order forms_____

Payment information _____ Souvenirs_____

Tickets/ticket wallets _____ Cash/Cash box_____

Security_____

Signs_____

Memorabilia:

Items list _____

_____

_____

_____

_____

_____

Display plans

Security_____ Storage_____

Delivery_____ Breakdown_____

At the Reunion Checklist

Souvenirs:
Registration kit souvenirs_____
To be distributed during the event_____
Sales information_____
Sales table/area
    Cash/Cash box_____ Displays_____
    Demonstration_____ AV Equipment_____
Sales table personnel
    Name _____ Shift _____
    Name _____ Shift _____
    Name _____ Shift _____
    Name _____ Shift _____
Security_____
Signs_____

Presentation/Entertainment:
Start time_____ End time_____
Description

People involved
  Name _____ Role_____
  Name _____ Role_____
  Name _____ Role_____
  Name _____ Role_____
AV equipment needed_____

Setup _____ Breakdown _____
Staff_____

Music:
Description _____
_____
Musicians/DJ_____
AV equipment needed_____ Power supply needed_____
Music start time_____ Music end time_____

Decorations:
Decorating plans

Supplies needed _____
_____
_____
_____
_____
Decorating start time_____ Decorating breakdown time_____

Event Notes

Accounts Settlement Sheet

Vendor _____

Deposit paid	_____
Amount calculator	

Item _____ # _____ x $_____ = _____
Item _____ # _____ x $_____ = _____
Item _____ # _____ x $_____ = _____
Item _____ # _____ x $_____ = _____
Item _____ # _____ x $_____ = _____

Total owed _____
Balance due _____
Amount paid _____
Paid by _____
Receipt _____

Vendor _____

Deposit paid	_____
Amount calculator	

Item _____ # _____ x $_____ = _____
Item _____ # _____ x $_____ = _____
Item _____ # _____ x $_____ = _____
Item _____ # _____ x $_____ = _____
Item _____ # _____ x $_____ = _____

Total owed _____
Balance due _____
Amount paid _____
Paid by _____
Receipt _____

Vendor _____

Deposit paid	_____
Amount calculator	

Item _____ # _____ x $_____ = _____
Item _____ # _____ x $_____ = _____
Item _____ # _____ x $_____ = _____
Item _____ # _____ x $_____ = _____
Item _____ # _____ x $_____ = _____

Total owed _____
Balance due _____
Amount paid _____
Paid by _____
Receipt _____

Ticket Reconciliation Sheet

Event _____

Tickets sold

Tickets pre-sold	_____
Tickets sold at-the-door	_____
Unsold tickets	_____
Total	_____ = _____ Total tickets printed

Ticket revenues

Ticket value_____ x number collected _____ = _____ amount collected

Ticket value_____ x number collected _____ = _____ amount collected

Ticket value_____ x number collected _____ = _____ amount collected

Ticket value_____ x number collected _____ = _____ amount collected

Ticket value_____ x number collected _____ = _____ amount collected

Total collected _____

Event _____

Tickets sold

Tickets pre-sold	_____
Tickets sold at-the-door	_____
Unsold tickets	_____
Total	_____ = _____ Total tickets printed

Ticket revenues

Ticket value_____ x number collected _____ = _____ amount collected

Ticket value_____ x number collected _____ = _____ amount collected

Ticket value_____ x number collected _____ = _____ amount collected

Ticket value_____ x number collected _____ = _____ amount collected

Ticket value_____ x number collected _____ = _____ amount collected

Total collected _____

Souvenir Sales Record Sheet

Souvenir Item _____

Beginning inventory _____ - number sold/given away _____ = _____ ending inventory

Price $_____ x number sold _____ = _____ amount collected

Souvenir Item _____

Beginning inventory _____ - number sold/given away _____ = _____ ending inventory

Price $_____ x number sold _____ = _____ amount collected

Souvenir Item _____

Beginning inventory _____ - number sold/given away _____ = _____ ending inventory

Price $_____ x number sold _____ = _____ amount collected

Souvenir Item _____

Beginning inventory _____ - number sold/given away _____ = _____ ending inventory

Price $_____ x number sold _____ = _____ amount collected

Souvenir Item _____

Beginning inventory _____ - number sold/given away _____ = _____ ending inventory

Price $_____ x number sold _____ = _____ amount collected

Souvenir Item _____

Beginning inventory _____ - number sold/given away _____ = _____ ending inventory

Price $_____ x number sold _____ = _____ amount collected

Souvenir Item _____

Beginning inventory _____ - number sold/given away _____ = _____ ending inventory

Price $_____ x number sold _____ = _____ amount collected

Souvenir Item _____

Beginning inventory _____ - number sold/given away _____ = _____ ending inventory

Price $_____ x number sold _____ = _____ amount collected

Souvenir Item _____

Beginning inventory _____ - number sold/given away _____ = _____ ending inventory

Price $_____ x number sold _____ = _____ amount collected

Total collected from souvenir sales $_____

Breakdown/Cleanup List

Event _____

Facility rules for cleanup

Decorations

    Items to keep_____

    Items to auction/giveaway_____

Memorabilia

    Items to keep_____

    Items to go to the next event_____

    Who will transport_____

    Items returned to lender_____

    Items to store _____

    Security_____

Food/Beverage

    Leftover instructions_____

    Containers _____

Entertainment

    Equipment returned to lender_____

    Equipment to store_____

    Security_____

Souvenirs

    Items to go to next event_____

    Who will transport _____

Photography

    Materials for committee _____

Videography

    Materials for committee _____

Notes

Chapter 31

Whew!!!
After the Reunion

Before you breathe a sigh of relief that the reunion is over, your work may not be done. You probably will have some last details to attend to, items to return, final payments to make and extra funds to disburse. You may want to get the committee together to celebrate your accomplishments and talk over the highlights of the reunion.

Most reunions have a few tasks left after the reunion is over. For those items that can wait a few days, let them wait — at least long enough to give your committee members a chance to relax and recuperate.

Return any items that you borrowed, such as props, decorations, utensils, AV equipment, photographs or memorabilia along with a thank you for the loan of the items.

Most of the bills should be taken care of before or during the reunion unless you negotiated credit terms. Take care of any outstanding payments as soon as possible.

After all the deposits have been collected and the final payments have been made, you may have to decide what to do with extra money or bank accounts. If you plan to invest, choose an instrument that matures at the time you'll plan the next reunion, so you'll have money available.

In this chapter you'll find information to help you clear up the final details — distribute souvenirs, send thank you's, return borrowed items, make final payments, account for any extra funds, evaluate the reunion and make plans for the next one.

Committee Pass Along List

Executive Chairman
- ☐ Committee meeting agendas
- ☐ Assignment calendar
- ☐ Sub-committee task sheets
- ☐ Registration kit example
- ☐ Reunion evaluations

Finance Chairman
- ☐ Final reunion budget
- ☐ Ledger of expenses and receipts
- ☐ Bank account information

Events Chairman
- ☐ Vendor interview sheets
- ☐ Vendor comparison sheets
- ☐ Fund-raiser information

Record Keeper
- ☐ Member data sheets
- ☐ Dated missing list
- ☐ Contributors list
- ☐ Reunion book sample
- ☐ Example of each mailing

Memorabilia Chairman
- ☐ Banners
- ☐ Logos
- ☐ Insignias
- ☐ Audio clips
- ☐ Film images
- ☐ Photographs
- ☐ Printed materials
- ☐ List of where each memorabilia item was obtained

Publicity Chairman
- ☐ Media contact list
- ☐ PR kits
- ☐ Public service announcements
- ☐ Newsreleases
- ☐ Posters
- ☐ Advertisements

Post-Reunion Souvenir Sales Record Sheet

Souvenir Item _____

Beginning inventory _____ - number sold _____ = _____ ending inventory

Price $ _____ x number sold _____ = _____ amount collected

Souvenir Item _____

Beginning inventory _____ - number sold _____ = _____ ending inventory

Price $ _____ x number sold _____ = _____ amount collected

Souvenir Item _____

Beginning inventory _____ - number sold _____ = _____ ending inventory

Price $ _____ x number sold _____ = _____ amount collected

Souvenir Item _____

Beginning inventory _____ - number sold _____ = _____ ending inventory

Price $ _____ x number sold _____ = _____ amount collected

Souvenir Item _____

Beginning inventory _____ - number sold _____ = _____ ending inventory

Price $ _____ x number sold _____ = _____ amount collected

Souvenir Item _____

Beginning inventory _____ - number sold _____ = _____ ending inventory

Price $ _____ x number sold _____ = _____ amount collected

Souvenir Item _____

Beginning inventory _____ - number sold _____ = _____ ending inventory

Price $ _____ x number sold _____ = _____ amount collected

Souvenir Item _____

Beginning inventory _____ - number sold _____ = _____ ending inventory

Price $ _____ x number sold _____ = _____ amount collected

Total amount collected $ _____
Remaining Inventory

    Item _____ Number _____

    Item _____ Number _____

    Item _____ Number _____

    Item _____ Number _____

    Item _____ Number _____

Accounting for the Money

Starting amount _____

Revenue

       Tickets sold _____ x $ _____ = _____
       Tickets sold _____ x $ _____ = _____
       Tickets sold _____ x $ _____ = _____
       Tickets sold _____ x $ _____ = _____
       Tickets sold _____ x $ _____ = _____
       Tickets sold _____ x $ _____ = _____
       Souvenirs sold _____ x $ _____ = _____
       Souvenirs sold _____ x $ _____ = _____
       Souvenirs sold _____ x $ _____ = _____
       Souvenirs sold _____ x $ _____ = _____
       Souvenirs sold _____ x $ _____ = _____
       Souvenirs sold _____ x $ _____ = _____

Total Revenue _____

Expenses

       Committee/overhead _____
       Printing/Mailing _____
       Website _____
       Locating missing members _____
       Facility rental _____
       Food/Beverage _____
       Entertainment _____
       Decorations/memorabilia _____
       Memorials _____
       Reunion Book _____
       Photography _____
       Videography _____
       CD-ROM _____
       Other souvenirs _____

Total Expenses _____

Remaining funds $ _____

Plans for the remaining funds:

Chapter 32

Waiting in the Wings:
Using a Professional Planner

*I*t may have occurred to you that someone could start a business as a professional reunion coordinator — and make money at it. There are such businesses! If you find that you can't do it *all* yourselves — even if you can't do most of it yourselves — there's professional support out there for you. Professional planning companies will act as your agent, hire services and vendors on your behalf and coordinate them during the reunion.

Reunion planners specialize in reunions. They help coordinate vendors such as bands and caterers. They reserve facilities, assist with the membership search and collect information from your members. They will print a memory (reunion) book, take a group photograph, design and mail invitations and plan publicity. They will collect payments directly from your group members and provide staffing for registration.

Companies that advertise themselves as event planners or event consultants offer party-planning services but typically don't become involved in helping with your member search, sending invitations or collecting payment directly from your members. Event planners' services include developing theme ideas, reserving facilities and coordinating services such as musicians, bar service, florists and caterers. Many large hotels or convention facilities have banquet managers or event planners on staff who perform similar services.

In this chapter you'll find information to help you find a company to hire and coordinate vendors so you won't have to. This chapter will help you determine when and how a professional planner can serve you best.

Signing a Contract with a Professional Planner

Consider the following before you negotiate a contract with a professional planner:

Precise description of service or product

- terms and limitations of service
- membership location plans
- documenting where information about members was received
- negotiations with facilities, caterers, musicians, videographers, photographers, souvenir providers, speakers, publicity plans, etc.
- a requirement that final lists of members be given to the committee after the reunion and not sold to marketing companies unless the membership agrees to it
- reunion book and graphics
- committee reimbursement
- publicity
- committee meeting calls
- in what form records from the reunion will be given to the committee
- require that staff from the company be labelled as staff
- staffing for each event
- how staff will dress during the reunion
- no client recruiting during the reunion
- whether the company will hire freelancers
- back up plans

Dates, places, times

- date(s) and time of each reunion event
- date and time for committee updates on progression of plans

Contact person

- contact person and phone number the firm
- name and phone number of the individual working with your group
- after hours or emergency number

Charges, fees, and deposits

- fees for each service
- prices to members for tickets
- what committee expenditures prior to hiring the company will be reimbursed
- what will be done with any fund-raising money gathered during the reunion
- any discounts that apply

Payment Schedule

- when deposits are due
- payments in installments
- when final payment is due
- interest (if charged)
- when deposit is returned if not applied to the final bill

Methods of payment accepted

- personal or committee checks, billing on account, credit cards, money order

Not to exceed clause

- put a limit on things such as secretarial services, locating services

Extra charges

- staff, telephone, travel or overtime

Cancellation Policy

- no penalties if you cancel before a specified date
- if you cancel, payment of actual expenses incurred only
- if they cancel, payment of expenses incurred in finding another professional planner

Deadlines or due dates

- when mailings will be sent
- when member search will begin and end (avoid terms such as 'best effort' or 'in a timely fashion,' try to get firm dates)

Deliveries or pickup

- who is responsible for delivery or pickup of any element of the reunion

Shipping method

- If anything is to be shipped to you, by which method -- USPS, UPS, registered, insured, overnight

Staffing or Equipment to be Used

- who will be in attendance during the reunion
- who will staff which events
- how the staff will be dressed
- whether problems or questions will be handled by the company or referred to the committee
- whether freelancers will be hired just for the day of the reunion

Staff's responsibilities

- who will oversee each event
- whether they will be there during the entire event
- who to contact for decisions during the reunion

Committee's responsibilities

- what information the committee will provide to the planner (membership lists, logos, mascots, originating organization contacts, etc.)
- which committee members are responsible for making last-minute decisions during the reunion

Non-Performance Penalty

- if one of the companies that the planner has hired does not perform, detail the planner's responsibility to replace that service with another, even if it might be more expensive

Professional Planner Interview Checklist

Company Name:

Address:

Contact Name: Phone: Fax:

E-mail: URL:

Things to take with you to the interview

Grand Plan _____

Vision for each event _____

Approximate budget_____

Your group's numbers_____

List of committee members _____

Planner's business history

Planner's portfolio

Event photographs _____

Invitation examples _____ Souvenir examples_____

Most successful reunion_____

Creativity_____ Unique celebrations_____

Pattern of events_____

Pricing structure_____

Finances

Publicity

Billing Data

    Deposit date _____ Deposit amount_____

    Deposit date _____ Deposit amount_____

    Final payment due _____ Final payment amount_____

    Payment methods accepted _____

Professional Planner Interview Checklist

Member search plans

Records management

Website access

Preferred facilities

Preferred vendors

Dispute resolution

Decoration plans

Memorabilia

Registration materials

Memorials

Reunion staffing

Backup plans

Chapter 33

A Reunion on the Road:
Travel and Transportation

ho says you can't take your reunion on the road? You *can* go around the world in 80 days ... on a cruise ship. Maybe you want to visit the home of your ancestors or the site of an historical event. Travel reunions are fun!

If you want to go on tour, you can plan a customized trip for your group and handle all of the details yourself, or you can find a tour operator to plan the trip for you. You may be looking for a tour for one of your reunion events or you may plan the entire reunion around touring together. Some tour packages include all services available at each destination — overnight accommodation, meals, flights, car rental, railway excursions, steamship cruises or motorcoach tours. Groups can benefit from significant discounts in each component of the trip, making overall costs reasonable.

You don't have to travel every day either. Arrange a day-long tour during the reunion or hop on a train for a leisurely day in the countryside. Cruise the coastal waters or do some sight-seeing as a group? Or, plan your reunion entirely around the transportation. Charter a boat or an airplane. Arrange for a private train. Even if you stay in one place, you may need transportation. Guests may need to go back and forth to the airport or to the different reunion venues.

In this chapter you'll find information to help you develop a reunion tour, and to show you how to work with ground, water, air and train transportation providers.

Transportation Possibilities Checklist

- [ ] ATVs
- [ ] Automobile
- [ ] Barges
- [ ] Bicycles
- [ ] Camels
- [ ] Canoes
- [ ] Carriages
- [ ] Catamarans
- [ ] Charter Jets
- [ ] Classic Cars
- [ ] Clippers
- [ ] Commercial Airlines
- [ ] Commuter Planes
- [ ] Commuter Trains
- [ ] Convertibles
- [ ] Cruise Ships
- [ ] Cutters
- [ ] Double-Decker Buses
- [ ] Ferries
- [ ] Fishing boats
- [ ] Galleys
- [ ] Gondolas
- [ ] Helicopters
- [ ] High-speed Railway
- [ ] Horse-drawn Carriages
- [ ] Horses
- [ ] Hot Air Balloons
- [ ] Houseboats
- [ ] Humvies
- [ ] Jeeps
- [ ] Junks

- [ ] Kayaks
- [ ] Ketches
- [ ] Lightrail
- [ ] Limosine
- [ ] Luxury Cars
- [ ] Motorboats
- [ ] Motorcoaches
- [ ] Open-air Trains
- [ ] Outrigger Canoes
- [ ] Private Trains
- [ ] Private Trains
- [ ] Recreation Vehicles
- [ ] Rickshaws
- [ ] Sailboats
- [ ] Sampans
- [ ] School Buses
- [ ] Schooners
- [ ] Sleds
- [ ] Sleighs
- [ ] Snowmobiles
- [ ] Steamboats
- [ ] Street Cars
- [ ] Subways
- [ ] Taxi
- [ ] Town Car
- [ ] Trolleys
- [ ] Trucks
- [ ] Vans
- [ ] Yachts
- [ ] Zodiacs

Tour Components Checklist

Objectives

Itinerary

Expenses

Transportation_____

Baggage handling_____

Lodging_____

Meals_____

Admissions_____

Taxes/Fees_____

Administration_____

Sponsors

Transportation

Air   From_____ To _____

Cost_____ Each_____

Air   From_____ To _____

Cost_____ Each_____

Ground   From_____ To _____

Cost_____ Each_____

Ground   From_____ To _____

Cost_____ Each_____

Ground   From_____ To _____

Cost_____ Each_____

Ground   From_____ To _____

Cost_____ Each_____

Water   From_____ To _____

Cost_____ Each_____

Rail   From_____ To _____

Cost_____ Each_____

Meals

Meal Plan_____

Area_____ Facility_____ Meal_____ Cost_____

Area_____ Facility_____ Meal_____ Cost_____

Area_____ Facility_____ Meal_____ Cost_____

Area_____ Facility_____ Meal_____ Cost_____

Area_____ Facility_____ Meal_____ Cost_____

Area_____ Facility_____ Meal_____ Cost_____

Lodging

Area_____ Facility_____ Check-in_____ Check-out_____

Single_____ Double_____ Deluxe_____ Family_____

Amenities_____

Area_____ Facility_____ Check-in_____ Check-out_____

Single_____ Double_____ Deluxe_____ Family_____

Amenities_____

Area_____ Facility_____ Check-in_____ Check-out_____

Single_____ Double_____ Deluxe_____ Family_____

Amenities_____

Area_____ Facility_____ Check-in_____ Check-out_____

Single_____ Double_____ Deluxe_____ Family_____

Amenities_____

Participant Items

Reading/resources_____

Name badges/lanyard_____

List of participants_____

Tour details_____

Passport/visa requirements_____

Currency exchange instructions_____

Gratuity guide_____

Arrival/departure procedures_____

Lodging check-in/check-out procedures_____

Tour Leader Items

Welcome-aboard announcements_____

Entertainment during transportation_____

Payment schedule_____

Payment rules_____

    items charged to the tour_____

    items responsible for by tour participants_____

Payments to vendors_____

    methods _____ when due_____

Payments to vendors_____

    methods _____ when due_____

Payments to vendors_____

    methods _____ when due_____

Tour Itinerary Checklist

Tour Name: _____ Contact Name: _____

Tour Group: _____ Contact Phone: _____

Date: _____ Transportation by: _____

Beginning: _____ Ending: _____

Destination: _____

Lodging: _____

Meals: _____

Arrive:	Depart:	Itinerary Sequence:	Description:

Tour Leader Checklist

Day-by-day itinerary
    Departure/arrival times
    Meeting places and times
    Meals: which are included, where served, menus, tipping guide
    Sight-seeing: admissions, guided or not, tipping guide, information brochures, maps
    Accommodations: facility, check-in procedures, room assignments, special requests
    Transportation: mode, check-in procedures, seating assignments

- [ ] Extra itineraries to give to passengers
- [ ] Passenger special request list
- [ ] General information sheet
- [ ] Rooming list for each hotel
- [ ] Tour Books for general information
- [ ] Vendor contact list
- [ ] Safety tips
- [ ] Payment log sheet
- [ ] Name badges
- [ ] Extra baggage tags
- [ ] Baggage allowance

- [ ] Hotel charges/check-out rules
- [ ] Emergency contact information
- [ ] Emergency medical information
- [ ] Audio/video entertainment
- [ ] Airport security measures reminder
- [ ] Arrival procedures
- [ ] Daily money guide
- [ ] Currency exchange explanation
- [ ] Embassy/Consulate list
- [ ] Common tourist scams explanation
- [ ] Baggage service procedures

Basic Packing List

- [ ] Reunion information
- [ ] Baggage allowance rules
- [ ] Passport/identification
- [ ] Copies of passport/driver's license
- [ ] Extra passport photos
- [ ] Traveler's checks, cash, credit card
- [ ] Tickets/reservations
- [ ] Travel alarm
- [ ] Fold-up luggage carrier
- [ ] All-weather coat/umbrella
- [ ] Extra batteries (clock, watch)
- [ ] Swiss Army knife/utensils
- [ ] Bungee cord/duct tape/nylon strap
- [ ] Luggage tags/locks
- [ ] Copy of prescriptions
- [ ] Keys
- [ ] Itinerary to leave at home

Basic First Aid Supplies

- [ ] Pain reliever/anti-inflammatory
- [ ] Upset stomach/diarrhea remedy
- [ ] Motion sickness remedy
- [ ] Antibiotic/hydrocortisone ointment
- [ ] Nasal spray
- [ ] Cough/cold medicine
- [ ] Band-aids/gauze
- [ ] Blister/foot remedy
- [ ] Antibacterial soap
- [ ] Alcohol wipes
- [ ] Contact lens solution/cleaner
- [ ] Sunburn remedy
- [ ] Daily prescriptions (+ extras)
- [ ] Extra eyeglass
- [ ] Medical information sheet
- [ ] List of drugs taken daily (+ generic names)
- [ ] Emergency contact numbers

Tour Operator Interview Checklist

Company Name:

Address:

Contact Name: Phone: Fax:

E-mail: URL:

Tour Operator's experience

Professional association memberships _____

Tour Services

     Transportation _____

     Meals _____

     Lodging _____

     Participant items _____

     Host responsibilities _____

     Tour insurance _____

     Venue tickets _____

     Fees _____

     Discounts/premiums _____

     Taxes _____

Tour length _____

Tour customized for the group _____

Tour brochures _____

Tour history _____

Client list/references

Tour itinerary

Billing Data

Deposit date _____ Deposit amount _____

Deposit date _____ Deposit amount _____

Final payment due _____ Final payment amount _____

Payment methods accepted _____

Signing a Contract with a Tour Operator

Consider the following before you negotiate a contract with a tour or travel operator:

Precise description of service or product

- terms and limitations of service
- tour itinerary
- all tour costs and what items are the responsibility of the participants
- the names and terms of service with all lodging facilities, meal providers, entertainment venues, transportation providers, and other service providers such as baggage handling services
- responsibilities of the staff accompanying the tour
- the list of items that will be given to participants
- travel insurance costs and coverage
- payment schedule
- pre-trip meetings with participants
- back up and contingency plans

Dates, places, times

- date(s), time and length of each tour event
- date and time for committee updates on tour preparations

Contact person

- contact person and phone number the firm
- name and phone number of the individual working with your group
- after hours or emergency number

Charges, fees, and deposits

- fees for each service
- prices to members for tour tickets and all extras
- any premiums that have been negotiated
- any discounts that apply

Payment Schedule

- when deposits are due
- payments in installments
- when final payment is due
- interest (if charged)
- when deposit is returned if not applied to the final bill

Methods of payment accepted

- personal or committee checks, billing on account, credit cards, money order

Not to exceed clause

- limit charges to participant tickets only

Extra charges

- any charges for extra services such as extended tours or sight-seeing trips not included in the main tour cost

Cancellation Policy

- no penalties if you cancel before a specified date
- if you cancel, payment of actual expenses incurred only
- if they cancel, payment of expenses incurred in finding another tour, or extra charges that you would pay for booking later

Deadlines or due dates

- when participant materials will be sent or given out
- if visas are required, when visa applications will be sent to participants

Deliveries or pickup

- who is responsible for delivery or pickup of any materials or tickets

Shipping method

- If anything is to be shipped to you, by which method -- USPS, UPS, registered, insured, overnight

Staffing or Equipment to be Used

- who will be in attendance during the tour
- whether problems or questions will be handled by the company or referred to the committee
- whether on-location freelancers will be used during the tour

Staff's responsibilities

- who will oversee each tour event
- who will be available to contact at the company office in the event of problems during the tour

Committee's responsibilities

- what information the committee will provide to the tour company (membership lists, logos, mascots, emergency contact information, etc.)
- which committee members will be the spokespersons for the group during the tour

Non-Performance Penalty

- if one of the companies that the planner has hired does not perform, detail the planner's responsibility to replace that service with another, even if it might be more expensive

Transportation Provider Interview Checklist

Company Name:

Address:

Contact Name: _____ Phone: _____ Fax: _____

E-mail: _____ URL: _____

Transportation provider's experience

Professional association memberships _____

Company credentials _____

Insurance _____

Safety record _____

Operator qualifications _____

Safety Equipment _____

Emergency plans _____

Trip details

Time _____ Distance _____

Stops _____

Vehicle description

Maximum number of passengers _____ Vehicle security _____

Child safety equipment _____

Vehicle amenities _____ Vehicle signage _____

Meals _____ Entertainment _____

Baggage restrictions _____ Staff _____

Fees

Adult _____ Children _____

Extra mileage _____ Extra time _____

Gratuities _____ Staff lodging/meals _____

Client list/references

Billing Data

Deposit date _____ Deposit amount _____

Deposit date _____ Deposit amount _____

Final payment due _____ Final payment amount _____

Payment methods accepted _____

Signing a Contract with a Transportation Provider

Consider the following before you negotiate a contract with a transportation provider:

Precise description of service or product

- terms and limitations of service
- trip details including time, distance and stops
- vehicle description including maximum number of passengers, vehicle safety equipment, child safety equipment and vehicle amenities
- All services including meals, entertainment and staff
- baggage restrictions
- company safety record and insurance status
- emergency plans
- operator qualifications
- back up plans

Dates, places, times

- date(s) and time of each trip
- date and time for committee updates on trip plans

Contact person

- contact person and phone number the company
- name and phone number of staff and vehicle operators working with your group
- after hours or emergency number

Charges, fees, and deposits

- fees for each person, adult and children
- where charges for mileage begin, at the pickup location or where the vehicle begins the trip
- deposits to reserve vehicles
- any discounts that apply

Payment Schedule

- when deposits are due
- payments in installments
- when final payment is due
- interest (if charged)
- when deposit is returned if not applied to the final bill

Methods of payment accepted

- personal or committee checks, billing on account, credit cards, money order

Not to exceed clause

- put a limit on things such as extra travel time as a result of traffic, construction or weather

Extra charges

- extra mileage charges
- gratuities
- entertainment fees
- lodging and meals for the vehicle operator or staff

Cancellation Policy

- no penalties if you cancel before a specified date
- if you cancel, payment of actual expenses incurred only
- if they cancel, payment of expenses incurred in finding another transportation provider

Deadlines or due dates

- all pickup and drop off times
- all approximate transportation times

Deliveries or pickup

- who is responsible for delivery or pickup of any materials to be taken along during the trip, or given to participants

Shipping method

- If anything is to be shipped to you, by which method -- USPS, UPS, registered, insured, overnight

Staffing or Equipment to be Used

- precise vehicle to be used
- vehicle operator
- staff in addition to the vehicle operator

Staff's responsibilities

- who to contact for decisions in the event of a problem during the trip

Committee's responsibilities

- what information the committee will provide to the transportation operator (membership lists, logos or mascots for vehicle signage, etc.)
- which committee members are responsible for making decisions during the trip

Non-Performance Penalty

- if a vehicle breaks down or is unavailable, what will be done to make up for substituting another vehicle

Chapter 34:

Hired Hands and Hired Guns:
Temporary Help and Security

lanning a reunion requires teamwork and so does coordinating all of the people you might need to help you during the reunion. Too often we see reunion committees underestimate the people needed and end up working every minute of the reunion rather than enjoying the success of their hard work. Line up as many volunteers as you can from friends and family and members coming in from out of town for jobs that only last a short period of time, a quick task here or there or for setup and cleanup — jobs that take place before or after the event. Keep group members and committee members (for the most part) free of the responsibility of 'during the event' tasks such as registration, security and sales tables. These jobs are perfect for hired temporary help.

At some of the best hotels, security is a priority because of the type of clientele that use these hotels. Most facilities where you might hold a reunion, however, will not have extra security personnel to assign to your reunion. You'll need to hire them. If you plan to collect cash, make payments to vendors in cash or display valuable items, hire some security. Risk and liabilities can never be completely eliminated, but they can be reduced and security personnel are one way to reduce your risk of loss. You may want off-duty uniformed or plainclothes police officers if you need to guard cash, but you may not need trained police officers to control access at the door or to collect tickets. If you don't feel you need armed or uniformed police to protect your reunion, contact a security agency. Security agencies can provide personnel with a wide variety of skills.

Staffing Needs Worksheet

Event _____
Starting time_____ Ending time _____
Setup_____ Cleanup_____
Registration staff_____ Greeters _____
Ticket takers_____ Security_____
Sales table staff_____ Other_____

Event _____
Starting time_____ Ending time _____
Setup_____ Cleanup_____
Registration staff_____ Greeters _____
Ticket takers_____ Security_____
Sales table staff_____ Other_____

Event _____
Starting time_____ Ending time _____
Setup_____ Cleanup_____
Registration staff_____ Greeters _____
Ticket takers_____ Security_____
Sales table staff_____ Other_____

Event _____
Starting time_____ Ending time _____
Setup_____ Cleanup_____
Registration staff_____ Greeters _____
Ticket takers_____ Security_____
Sales table staff_____ Other_____

Event _____
Starting time_____ Ending time _____
Setup_____ Cleanup_____
Registration staff_____ Greeters _____
Ticket takers_____ Security_____
Sales table staff_____ Other_____

Event _____
Starting time_____ Ending time _____
Setup_____ Cleanup_____
Registration staff_____ Greeters _____
Ticket takers_____ Security_____
Sales table staff_____ Other_____

Event _____
Starting time_____ Ending time _____
Setup_____ Cleanup_____
Registration staff_____ Greeters _____
Ticket takers_____ Security_____
Sales table staff_____ Other_____

Temporary Agency Interview Checklist

Company Name:	
Address:	
Contact Name:	Phone: Fax:
E-mail:	URL:

Temporary agency's experience

Professional association memberships _____

Personnel

Specialties_____
Training _____
Hours available _____
Special skills needed _____

Agency's credentials

Worker's compensation _____
Guarantees _____
Fidelity bonding _____
Liability insurance _____

Fees

Client list/references

Billing Data

Deposit date _____ Deposit amount_____

Deposit date _____ Deposit amount_____

Final payment due _____ Final payment amount_____

Payment methods accepted _____

Signing a Contract with a Temporary Agency

Consider the following before you negotiate a contract with a temporary agency

Precise description of service or product
- terms and limitations of service
- staffing specialties
- training provided to staff
- worker's compensation insurance, fidelity bonding, liability insurance
- hours staff available
- specialized skills available
- guarantees
- back up plans

Dates, places, times
- date(s) and time of each reunion event
- date and time staff must be available for training and shifts

Contact person
- contact person and phone number the firm
- name and phone number of the individual working with your group
- after hours or emergency number

Charges, fees, and deposits
- fees for each staff member
- any deposit required to secure staff
- any discounts that apply

Payment Schedule
- when deposits are due
- payments in installments
- when final payment is due
- interest (if charged)
- when deposit is returned if not applied to the final bill

Methods of payment accepted
- personal or committee checks, billing on account, credit cards, money order

Not to exceed clause
- put a limit on the total number of hours staff will be available

Extra charges
- travel expenses

Cancellation Policy
- no penalties if you cancel before a specified date
- if you cancel, payment of actual expenses incurred only
- if they cancel, payment of expenses incurred in finding staff for each event

Deadlines or due dates
- when staff will be available for work or training

Deliveries or pickup
- who is responsible for delivery or pickup of any information relating to the staffing of the reunion

Shipping method
- If anything is to be shipped to you, by which method -- USPS, UPS, registered, insured, overnight

Staffing or Equipment to be Used
- staff members
- any equipment that the staff is required to provide

Staff's responsibilities
- responsibility for skills training prior to the reunion
- company's responsibility to provide bonded employees if they will be handling money
- who to contact for decisions in the event or problems

Committee's responsibilities
- what information the committee will provide to the temporary agency (skills needed, specialized skills needed, time staff to be available, place staff needs to be and duration of events)
- which committee members are responsible for making decisions regarding the staff during the reunion

Non-Performance Penalty
- if staff members do not perform, what the company will do to provide different or additional staff, or adjust the cost to reflect the loss of staff work

Security Firm Interview Checklist

Company Name:		
Address:		
Contact Name:	Phone:	Fax:
E-mail:	URL:	

Security firm's experience

Professional association memberships _____

Security firm's credentials

Security license _____
Fidelity bond _____
Liability insurance _____
Worker's compensation insurance _____

Personnel

Security Training _____
Emergency Training _____
Qualifications _____
Equipment provided _____
Policies _____

Fees

Client list/references

Billing Data

Deposit date _____ Deposit amount _____
Deposit date _____ Deposit amount _____
Final payment due _____ Final payment amount _____
Payment methods accepted _____

Signing a Contract with a Security Firm

Consider the following before you negotiate a contract with a security firm

Precise description of service or product

- terms and limitations of service
- current security license
- staff training and qualifications
- policies for dealing with situations such as intoxicated patrons or theft
- equipment provided by the security personnel
- emergency training
- fidelity bonds, liability insurance and worker's compensation insurance
- back up plans

Dates, places, times

- date(s) and time of each reunion event
- date and time security personnel will be available for training or work

Contact person

- contact person and phone number the firm
- name and phone number of the individual(s) working with your group
- after hours or emergency number

Charges, fees, and deposits

- fees for security personnel
- deposits
- any discounts that apply

Payment Schedule

- when deposits are due
- payments in installments
- when final payment is due
- interest (if charged)
- when deposit is returned if not applied to the final bill

Methods of payment accepted

- personal or committee checks, billing on account, credit cards, money order

Not to exceed clause

- put a limit on total time security personnel will be available and fees charged

Extra charges

- travel, meals or overtime

Cancellation Policy

- no penalties if you cancel before a specified date
- if you cancel, payment of actual expenses incurred only
- if they cancel, payment of expenses incurred in finding additional security personnel

Deadlines or due dates

- when security staff will be available for training and work

Deliveries or pickup

- who is responsible for delivery or pickup of any materials related to reunion security

Shipping method

- If anything is to be shipped to you, by which method -- USPS, UPS, registered, insured, overnight

Staffing or Equipment to be Used

- who will be in attendance during the reunion
- who will staff which events
- how the staff will be dressed
- whether problems or questions will be handled by the company or referred to the committee
- what equipment security personnel will be responsible for providing during the reunion

Staff's responsibilities

- who will oversee the security staff for each event
- whether the security staff will be in attendance during the entire event
- who to contact for decisions during the reunion in the event of problems

Committee's responsibilities

- what information the committee will provide to the security firm (items that need to be secured, security plans, where items or cash will be secured, additional security plans during the event)
- which committee members are responsible for making decisions during the reunion regarding security

Non-Performance Penalty

- if a theft or loss occurs in spite of security personnel, what measures will be taken to remedy the loss

Index

Index

Order Your Copy Today!

Reunion Solutions
IBSN 0-9724975-9-5
$26.95 + $3.75 S&H

_____ _____
Quantity   Cost

**Reunion Solutions on
CD-ROM**
IBSN 0-9724975-4-4
$18.95 + $3.75 S&H

_____ _____
Quantity   Cost

Reunion Solutions Planner
ISBN 0-9724975-8-7
$24.95 + $3.75 S&H

_____ _____
Quantity   Cost

**Reunion Solutions Planner
on CD-ROM**
ISBN 0-9724975-3-6
$16.95 + $3.75 S&H

_____ _____
Quantity   Cost

Celebration Solutions
ISBN 0-9724975-6-0
$26.95 + $3.75 S&H

_____ _____
Quantity   Cost

**Celebration Solutions on
CD-ROM**
ISBN 0-9724975-1-X
$18.95 + $3.75 S&H

_____ _____
Quantity   Cost

**Reunion Solutions Idea
Deck**
ISBN 0-9724975-7-9
$24.95 + $3.75 S&H

_____ _____
Quantity   Cost

**Reunion Solutions Idea
Deck on CD-ROM**
ISBN 0-9724975-2-8
$16.95 + $3.75 S&H

_____ _____
Quantity   Cost

SPECIAL SALE:
Buy all 4 printed books and Save $25.00
All 4 Books for **$75 + $15 S&H**

CO Residents add 3.5% sales tax _____

TOTAL_____

**Reunion Solutions on
CD-ROM: All 4 Reunion-
Planning titles on 1 CD**
ISBN 0-9724975-0-1
$49.95 + $3.75 S&H

_____ _____
Quantity   Cost

Name:_____

Address:_____

City:_____ ST:_____ Zip:_____

Phone:_____ E-mail:_____

Send payment to:

Reunion Solutions Press
P.O. Box 999, Niwot, CO 80544

Place your order online at:
www.ReunionSolutions.com